Free Stuff

FOR

Crafty Kids

ON THE

INTERNET

Judy Heim and Gloria Hansen

C&T PUBLISHING

Copyright © 1999 Judy Heim and Gloria Hansen
Developmental Editor: Beate Nellemann
Technical Editor: Barbara Konzak Kuhn
Cover and Book Design: Christina Jarumay
Front Cover Illustration: Christina Jarumay and Alan McCorkle © C&T Publishing
Illustrations: ©1999 Christina Jarumay

Library of Congress Cataloging-in-Publication Data
Heim, Judy.
   Free Stuff for crafty kids on the Internet / Judy Heim and Gloria Hansen.
   p. cm.
   Includes bibliographical references and index.
   ISBN 1-51712-008-00 (paper trade)
   1.Handicraft ——Computer Network resources Directories. 2.
Children's web sites Directories. 3. Free materials — Computer Network
resources Directories. I. Hansen, Gloria. II. Title.
TT11   .45 1999
025.06'7455—dc21

                                        99-6530
                                        CIP

Published by C&T Publishing, Inc.
P.O. Box 1456
Lafayette, CA 94549

Printed in Hong Kong
10 9 8 7 6 5 4 3 2

DEDICATION

We dedicate this book to moms and dads everywhere who indulge their children's need to be creative, showering them with crayons, buying them clay, and driving halfway across town just to buy the perfect brand of sidewalk chalk. Also we dedicate this book to our parents, who certainly indulged us.

Judy & Gloria

There are many, many great Web sites for kids. It's no surprise that the books chronicling them often swell as thick as a phone book. But we've scuttled the Internet to come up with a selection of Web sites that we think will inspire kids (and hopefully parents too) to be creative. But that doesn't mean there aren't many other sites that are equally illuminating and valuable. Also, because of the fluid nature of the Internet, it is inevitable that some of the Web sites listed may have moved or even vanished. Had we included only those Web sites that are sure to be around next year, this book wouldn't be nearly as valuable. If a URL doesn't get you to a Web site, don't be discouraged. Try another. Or read our tips for finding a Web site when its URL has seemingly vanished. We hope you and your child will use this book as a starting point for a creative journey that will enrich both of your lives and spirits.

Symbols in this book

 This icon signifies a bit of Judy-and-Gloria hard-earned wisdom—in other words, something we wished we knew when we first started surfing the Web.

 When you see this icon, read carefully—and don't make one of the same silly mistakes we have!

 This icon means that the Web site also sells products that relate to the information on their site.

Table of
Contents

1 Kids, Crafts, and Family Fun on the **WEB!** 6

- Taming America Online 6
- Anatomy of a Web Browser 9
- How to Tap Into a Web Page 11
- Common Error Messages When You Enter a Web Address 13
- Find Your Way Around the Web Without Getting Lost............15
- How to Use Bookmarks 16
- How to Print Web Pages or Selections from Web Pages 17
- How to Save Web Pages to Your Computer's Disk 19
- How to Capture Images You Find on the Internet....................21
- Get the Music and Animation Rolling!.....................................22
- Plug-In Troubleshooting 25
- Downloading and Installing Plug-Ins.......................................28
- Making the Internet Safe for Your Kids—and for Yourself 29
- Keeping Kids Safe on America Online 33
- Web Browsers Offer Web Site Screening,
  but Kid Screening Software Is Still Best..................................35
- Will My Computer Catch a Virus 37
- Web Searchers that Are Safe for Kids to Use 38

2 free Big Arts and Crafts Sites for the Whole Family 40

3 more free Collections of Kids' Craft Project Instructions 50

4 free Coloring Pages and Craft How-Tos from
the Web Sites of TV Shows and Cartoons..................................61

5 Web Sites with free Coloring Pages...........................68

6 free How-Tos for Making Stuff with Paper.................76

7 free How-Tos for Making Paper Dolls and Accessories...........84

8 free How-Tos for Making Paper Airplanes and Kites.......88

9 free Origami How-Tos..95

10 free Drawing and Art History Lessons for
Budding Artists...99

11 free Rubber Stamping and Scrapbooking Fun.........108

12 free Tole Painting and Decoupage Tutorials...............114

13 free Polymer Clay, Beading, and
Jewelry-Making How-Tos..120

14 free How-Tos for Puppet Making, Balloon Twisting,
Juggling, and Magic....................................125

15 free Holiday Crafting How-Tos..........................132

16 free Stitching How-Tos for Kids.......................148

17 free How-Tos for Candlemaking, Basket Weaving,
and Nature Crafts...154

18 free Help for Making (and Repairing) Teddy Bears.......161

19 free Help for Doll Makers and Lovers...........165

About the Authors..................................174

Index...175

Free Stuff on the Internet Series....176

Kids, Crafts, and Family

Fun on the Web!

" It's rarely a linear path that leads one from the decision to have children to an afternoon spent heating jellied seaweed on the kitchen stove," marveled one dad after a Saturday spent helping his daughter with a craft project. (Or was it a science project? These days it's sometimes hard to tell.)

When we were kids (yes, young readers, here comes that spiel) craft projects with Mom and Dad meant snipping snowflakes from paper or folding pages of the Sears Catalog to make angels. But today kids are into everything: rubber-stamping, decoupage, basket weaving, tole painting, and interior decorating. If you're a parent you know that sometimes it's hard to keep up.

That's why we've written this book. The Web offers parents and kids lots of craft project ideas, from how-tos for decorating T-shirts to suggestions for making party decorations, from illustrations for folding origami to instructions for twisting balloons into animal shapes. Web sites of popular kids' TV shows are often rich with ideas on how to spend a creative afternoon with your child.

But this book isn't just for kids. While we were writing it many of our adult friends confided that they would read it simply to learn many of the crafts that their kids or their friends' kids were already enjoying.

◎ TAMING AMERICA ONLINE

If you're like most American families you're probably on America Online. If not you can get a startup disk by calling 800/827-6364, or have a friend download the software for you from the Web (http://www.aol.com).

To get to the Internet from America Online, once you've installed the software and have connected to the service, press Ctrl-K, or Command-K on a Mac, and type the keyword INTERNET <ENTER> or WEB<ENTER>, and you're on the Internet.

Or, you can type Web page URLs—you know, those strings that begin with http://www...—into the location bar at the top of AOL's screen.

Use a Different Web Browser with America Online
Internet Explorer comes with some versions of America Online's software, but you can use Netscape Navigator instead if you prefer (and many people do). Here's how: dial up AOL and make the connection. Minimize America Online's software. Fire up Navigator. Type the Web address you want to head to and you're there.

Connect to America Online Through Your Internet Service Provider
You probably connect to America Online by calling a local phone number. But you can also tap in through your Internet service provider if you have one. Maybe AOL's phone number is a long-distance call for you. Or maybe you access the Internet through cable or satellite. AOL's normal rates still apply when you tap in this way, but you'll be avoiding long-distance phone charges if you normally incur them to call AOL.

In America Online 4.0, click the Setup button on the Sign-on screen. Select "Create a location for use with new access phone numbers or an ISP." Click Next. Select "Add a custom connection (for example TCP/IP)." Click Next. Now, when you go back to the Sign-on screen you should be able to choose from calling AOL via an AOL phone number or an "ISP/LAN Connection." You make the selection in the drop-down box under "Select Location." Now, connect to your Internet service, as you normally would, then fire up AOL's software and from the Sign-on screen select "ISP/LAN Connection."

You'll find crafts galore in the Kids Only area on America Online. To get there click on the Kids Only icon on the main AOL screen or type the keywords "kids only" into the location bar. Then click on the Art Studio.

In AOL's Kids Only Art Studio you'll find a library of craft projects, plus games and more.

⊚ ANATOMY OF A WEB BROWSER

Whether you tap into the Web through America Online, an Internet service provider, or a cable or satellite connection, the software centerpiece of your Web surfing will be what's called a browser. In the old days you needed different sorts of software to do different things on the Net. For instance, you needed mail software to send and receive e-mail; a newsreader to read public discussions; you needed special software called FTP for "file download protocol" to download files to your computer. Plus you needed a browser to view (or browse through) the graphical portion of the Internet known as the Web. Now all those functions are built into browsers.

Most computers are sold with Netscape's Navigator or Microsoft's Internet Explorer already installed. You can also download them for free from Netscape's Web site (**http://www.netscape.com**) or Microsoft's site (**http://www.microsoft.com**).

While you can use just about any computer to log onto the Internet in some fashion (even an original Apple II circa 1979), to be able to view graphics you'll need a computer manufactured in at least the last 8 years. If you have an older computer download a copy of the $35 Opera browser (**http://www.operasoftware.com**) which will run on any Windows 3.x-running PCs as old as 386SX's with 6 megabytes of RAM.

If you're running an older Macintosh, head to Chris Adams' Web Browsers for Antique Macs web page (**http://www.edprint.demon.co.uk/se/macweb.html**) and download Tradewave's MacWeb or an early version of NCSA Mosaic.

If you've never configured Internet software before, you'll need someone to help you, even if you're a computer genius (believe us, we know). Your ISP will (or should) give you directions on how to set up Windows 95/98 or the Macintosh OS to at least log on to their service.

But once you're connected, you're pretty much on your own. That's why we've put together this little tutorial.

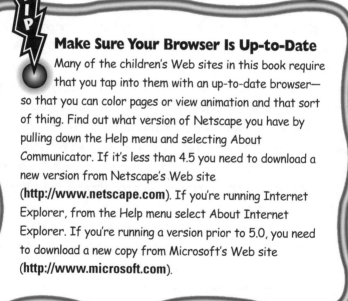

Make Sure Your Browser Is Up-to-Date

Many of the children's Web sites in this book require that you tap into them with an up-to-date browser—so that you can color pages or view animation and that sort of thing. Find out what version of Netscape you have by pulling down the Help menu and selecting About Communicator. If it's less than 4.5 you need to download a new version from Netscape's Web site (**http://www.netscape.com**). If you're running Internet Explorer, from the Help menu select About Internet Explorer. If you're running a version prior to 5.0, you need to download a new copy from Microsoft's Web site (**http://www.microsoft.com**).

Note: *The following directions are for Explorer 4.0 and 5.0 and Navigator 4.x but most will also work with previous versions of the browsers.*

◎ HOW TO TAP INTO A WEB PAGE

When your cursor changes to a hand, click on the object in order to be sent to a new page.

To get to a Web page, type its address, also known as its URL, or Universal Resource Locator, into the Address: bar in Navigator, or the Location: bar in Internet Explorer. (In older Web browsers you must preface the address with http: as in **http://www.paperdolls.org**, but in new browsers you can type simply **www.paperdolls.org**, or even **paperdolls.org**.)

Take note that the case of the letters is important, whether all the letters are upper case or lower case, or a combination of both.

You can also cut and paste URLs from other documents into the address or location bar. (Highlight the address with your mouse, press Ctrl-C, or Command-C on a Mac, then place the mouse in the location bar and press Ctrl-V, or Command-V on a Mac, to paste it in. Then hit <ENTER>.)

To move to other pages in the Web site, click on highlighted words, or, whenever your mouse cursor changes into a hand when its positioned on an object, right-click your mouse to go there.

How to Find the Web Site if the Web Page Isn't There

URLs point you to directories on a remote computer just like directory paths (**c:\windows\programs**) get you to different directories and subdirectories on your computer's hard disk.

If a Web address doesn't get you to what you want, try working back through the URL. For example, the Sesame Street Web site (**http://www2.ctw.org**) offers directions on how to create a family mobile with photos and a "magic stick" at this URL:

http://www2.ctw.org/celebrate/athome/article/0,1439,7206,00.html

But if it's not there, try working back through the URL and head to this address instead:

http://www2.ctw.org/celebrate/athome/article

Oh-oh! This address gives you a "server error." But don't be daunted. Try this instead:

http://www2.ctw.org/celebrate/athome

That should take you to the Try This at Home Page full of crafts. But say that the URL is gone. Why not try this:

http://www2.ctw.org/celebrate

That URL will take you to the Activity Time main page. But if worst comes to worst, you can also try this:

http://www2.ctw.org

Now, finally, you'll end up at the main Web page of the Children's Television Workshop, the home of Kermit, Miss Piggy, and the gang. This "root" URL is what's called a "registered domain." Registered domains usually don't change.

What does all that gobbledygook in a URL mean?

The http: tells your Internet service what kind of document you are trying to access on the Internet. HTTP stands for "hyper-text transfer protocol," the protocol of the Web. You might run into ftp: which stands for "file transfer protocol," an early Internet scheme for transferring files. The protocol is always followed by // which separates it from the document's address.

Next comes the domain name, for example, **www.disney.com**. The triple-w designates Disney's Web subdirectory on its Internet server. The .com suffix indicates that Disney is a commercial entity. If Disney were a college (don't we wish?) it would have an .edu suffix or an .org one if it were a non-profit. The words that following the domain name, separated by slashes, designate further subdirectories. Many, though not all, URLs end with a specific file name.

COMMON ERROR MESSAGES WHEN YOU ENTER A WEB ADDRESS

404 NOT FOUND
The requested URL /blocks/tips.html was not found on this server.

Reason: Your browser was able to find the Internet service or the computer on which the Web site was or is hosted, but no such page was found on the service. (The very last "word", at the end of a URL is the page's address. For example "tips.html"). Maybe the Web site owner removed that particular page. Or perhaps the Web site no longer exists.

Fix: Try working back through the URL as explained on page 12, to see if you can locate the Web site, or determine if the site itself is gone from the service. Also, try suffixing the page's address with "htm" or "html" instead of its current extension. For example, in place of TIPS.HTML type TIPS.HTM. (An HTML suffix is the same as an HTM, but some Web page hosting services require that Web pages be named with one or the other. Typing the wrong extension is a common mistake.)

DNS LOOKUP FAILURE or UNABLE TO LOCATE THE SERVER. The server does not have a DNS entry.

Reason: DNS stands for "domain name server." A domain name is the first part of a URL—for instance, in **www.ctpub.com**, ctpub.com is the domain name. Every Internet service (and AOL) has a database of such Web page host addresses. When you type a URL, the first thing your browser does is tell your Internet service to look up the domain name in its database, to find out where it's located. If it can't find it, your Internet service's computer may poll other domain name directories around the Internet to determine if any of them know where the domain name can be found. If none of them do, you may get the error message "DNS Lookup Failure."

Why can't they find the domain name? Maybe it no longer exists. Or perhaps it's so new that the domain name databases your Internet service uses can't find it. Sometimes you also get this error message when there's heavy traffic on the Internet. Your Internet service is taking too long to look up the name, so your browser errors out.

Fix: Try typing the URL into your browser later in the day. If you still get the error message, try the URL a few days or even a week later. If you still get error messages, assume the domain name no longer exists.

✋ NO RESPONSE FROM SERVER

Reason: Your browser is unable to get a timely response from the Web site's host computer. This can be because of heavy traffic on the Internet or on the branch of the Internet you are traveling. It can be because the computer that's hosting the Web site is overloaded (everyone is tapping in). Or it can be because your Internet service is overloaded, or its own computers are experiencing slowdowns for technical reasons.

Fix: Try the URL either in a few minutes, or later in the day.

◎ FIND YOUR WAY AROUND THE WEB WITHOUT GETTING LOST

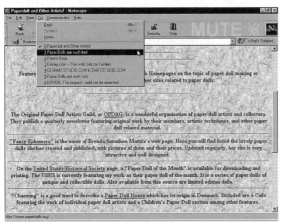

Lucinda's Paper Doll Web site offers a directory of links to other paper doll sites around the Web. But if you click on them, how will you find your way back to Lucinda's? There are several ways.

• Click the "Back" button in your browser to return to previously visited Web sites.

• Click the "History" button or select the history feature from a drop-down menu to list previously visited URLs.

• Or click your browser's drop-down location box, which displays the last dozen or so URLs that you have actually typed into the browser (in other words, it doesn't display links that you've clicked on something to get to).

◎ HOW TO USE BOOKMARKS

Web browsers let you "bookmark" sites so that you can visit
them again simply by fishing through your bookmark catalog.
You usually just click a bookmark icon (or "Favorites" in Internet
Explorer) or select the feature from a toolbar to add the Web
site that you're currently visiting to your bookmark list.

**You Can Add Shortcuts to Web Sites on Your Windows
Desktop.** Say there's a particular Web site you like to visit
everyday. If you're running Windows 95/98 you can add a shortcut to it from your desktop. When you click on the shortcut icon
your browser will load, dial your Internet service, and send you to
the Web site. Holding down your mouse's button, drag the site
from a link in a Web page. Or, if you're using Internet Explorer,
drag from the Address bar to the left of the Links bar or the
Favorites menu. If you're using Netscape, drag the icon to the left
of Location: when a page is loaded. Your mouse cursor should
change into a circle with a slash as you drag the URL to the desktop.

**You Can Customize Your Browser's Personal Toolbar
by Adding Bookmarks.** You can customize the personal
toolbar in Communicator or the Links bar in Internet
Explorer, by adding not only icons for frequently visited
URLs, but also folders of bookmarks. In Communicator add a
URL to the personal toolbar by dragging a link from a Web
page or by dragging the icon to the left of Location: when a
page is loaded. To add a folder instead to the personal toolbar click the Bookmarks icon, select "Edit Bookmarks" and
highlight the folder you wish to place on the toolbar. Right-
click and select "Set as Toolbar Folder." In Internet Explorer
you can similarly customize the Links bar by adding individual
URLs as well as folders. Drag folders from the Favorites
menu to add them to the Links bar. To add a URL to the link
bar drag it from the Address bar to the left of the Links
bar, from the Favorites menu or from a Web page.

You Can Use Third-Party Bookmark Software to Organize Your Bookmarks. There are a lot of low-cost utilities for organizing bookmarks that you can download from the Web. These are particularly handy if you're using two browsers—both Netscape and Internet Explorer for example. They enable you to store your bookmarks in a central location, and organize them into folders with icons—and in a more efficient manner than you can in your browser. Some utilities also let you password protect bookmarks. A good spot to download them is C/net's Shareware.Com (**http://www.shareware.com**). Search for the phrase"bookmark organizer." For PCs we like the free program LinkMan from Thomas Reimann. For Macs we like URL Manager Pro, the $25 shareware program from Alco Blom (**http://www.url-manager.com**).

◎ HOW TO PRINT WEB PAGES OR SELECTIONS FROM WEB PAGES

You can print entire Web pages just like you'd print any other document on your computer screen.

First, wait until the page is transmitted completely to your computer. In Navigator you'll see what looks like snow falling through the big 'N' logo in the top right-hand corner of the screen. If you're using a Mac you'll see shooting stars. That means the page is being transmitted to your computer. In Explorer, the 'e' logo in the top right-hand corner spins as the page is downloading. When it stops, the page is complete.

To print in Navigator, pull down the File menu and select Print Preview. Once you click the Print button in the Preview window, you'll get a dialog box in which you can choose which pages of the currently viewed Web page you wish to print. On a Macintosh, pull down the File menu and select Print.

In Internet Explorer, pull down the File menu and select Print.

On more complex Web sites your browser might ask you to specify which frame you'd like to print. A frame is a division of the page (a page with multiple frames is usually framed by multiple scroll bars). You will need to go back to the page and click on the side or section you wish to print then head back to the printing menu to print it.

Internet Explorer gives you the option of printing just the selected frame, all the frames on the Web page, or the entire Web page as you see it in your browser.

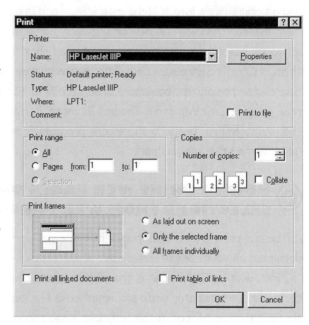

You can also print sections of a Web page by highlighting with your mouse the sections you wish to print, copying your selection into the clipboard, then pasting it into your word processor and printing it there.

Remember, Web Pages Are Copyrighted! Web pages are copyrighted just as any publication is. You should not print them except for your own personal use without asking permission from the Web page's owner. The same holds true for any elements on the page, including text but also graphics. Never, ever print or distribute these things—or, heaven forbid, put them on your own Web page. If you want to print multiple copies for use in a children's class or at a children's party, please ask the Web page owner for permission first.

◎ HOW TO SAVE WEB PAGES TO YOUR COMPUTER'S DISK

You can save entire Web pages to your disk so that you can peruse them later, but keep in mind the warning—these pages are copyrighted and you should not distribute them.

First the page must be completely loaded.
Remember to click on the frame you wish to save.

In your browser, select Save as... from the File menu. A pop-up box will give you a choice of saving the page as HTML or text. If you're using a Mac, the pop-up box will give you the option of saving the text as source, which is the same as HTML.

HTML is the coding that is used to format Web pages—it's similar to text, but with a few weird notations thrown in. Save the page in HTML format if you plan to view it later with your browser while you're off-line. (To view it in your browser later, from the File menu select Open Page. On a Mac, select Open Page in Navigator. Click Choose File, and then click your way to the file stored on your hard disk. Once you've found it, click the Open button.)

If you want to merely pull up the Web page's text in your word processor, and perhaps print it later, save it as Text.

Neither of these features will let you save the page's images, however. To save the graphics you need to:
Position your cursor over each image you wish to save, and right-click. On a Mac, click-hold. A menu box will pop up. Select Save Image As... or Save Picture As... . Save it into the same directory as you saved the page's HTML code.

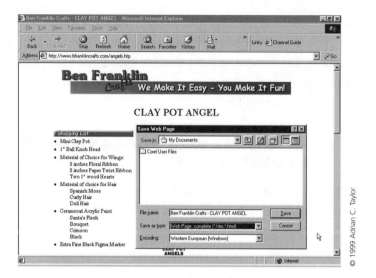

Your browser will let you save Web pages either as plain text or with their HTML formatting, but neither option will save graphics. You'll need to save each image individually.

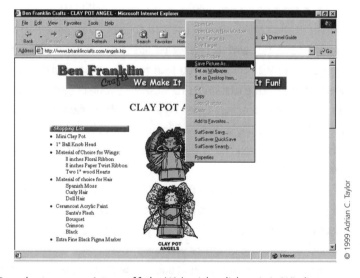

In order to save a picture off the Web, right click on it in Windows or click-hold on a Mac and select Save as... . Remember though that these images are copyrighted by their artist and you should not print or distribute them without asking permission first.

◎ HOW TO CAPTURE IMAGES YOU FIND ON THE INTERNET

Images on Web pages are copyrighted just like text is. If you want to use them in any way—either to print to distribute to your friends or post on your own Web pages—the same rules apply as to text: you need to ask the owner's permission first!

Position your cursor over the image and right-click. On a Mac click-hold. A menu box will pop up. Select Save Image As or Save Picture As...

You can later view it in either your browser or a graphics program like Paint Shop Pro. You can even import it into a word processing document. (In Microsoft Word, from the Insert menu select Picture.)

Can't Find a Picture That You've Saved to Your Disk? It happens all the time. You click on an image on the Web to save it to your computer, and then you can't find it after it's saved. If you can't remember the name of the graphic that you saved, go back to the Web page and click on it again to see the name. Then, if you have a PC running Windows 95/98, click Start, then Find and type the name of the file. Windows will find it for you.

If you have a Mac, type the name of the file in "Find File" or "Sherlock" (under the Apple Menu), and your Mac will find it for you.

TIP

Use SurfSaver to Save Web Pages for Future Viewing Say you're planning a kids party and have found a gaggle of Web sites that offer directions for craft projects and games. You're thinking of printing the pages—maybe making multiple copies to pass out to the kids. But of course, you'll need permission from the Web site owners to do that. But wait! There's a better way than wasting all that printer ink. SurfSaver from askSam Systems (**http://www.surfsaver.com**) is a $29.95 shareware utility that integrates with your browser enabling you to save and catalog Web pages for later viewing off-line. You can search pages and view them, complete with graphics and links, without even tapping into the Net. SurfSaver works with versions 4.0 and later of Internet Explorer and Netscape. Mac users can have the same fun with Web Devil, a $10 shareware program from Bob Bradley and Chaotic Software (**http:www.chaoticsoftware.com**). It requires System 7.5 or higher and a browser. Both Windows and Mac users can also try a demo of the commercial program Web Buddy from DataViz, Inc. (**http.www.dataviz.com**).

GET THE MUSIC AND ANIMATION ROLLING!

"Mom! Why isn't the music playing?" your tike cries. "When daddy was at the computer it was playing Twinkle, Twinkle Little Star!"

Well, fine, the computer always works for daddy, you huff, but not for mom.

Or maybe your household is more like ours where our husbands grumble: "Why does the computer always work for my wife but not for me?"

The most important thing to remember in getting the music and video rolling is that your computer is not some sprawling home multi-media center that puts you at the mercy of cables snaking all over the floor. Usually there's some little piece of software that's at fault. More than likely it's something called a plug-in.

A plug-in is something you plug into your browser, a small helper application. Plug-ins play movie clips or music, and sometimes animation. They run or display files that your browser encounters on the Web that it would otherwise not know what to do with.

Most plug-ins works with both Internet Explorer and Netscape. Many probably came with your browser, already plugged in, so to speak. All the important plug-ins are free for downloading from the Web. (In fact when a Web site requires that your browser has a particular plug-in in order to play or display something, it will usually include a link where you may download it.)

If your browser is unable to play a sound on a Web page, for instance, it's probably because it lacks the appropriate plug-in to play the sound file. There are many types of sound files—WAV, MIDI, AIF, to name a few. A Web page might have any of them, and your browser will need to know what to do with such a file in order to play it.

Make Sure Java and Javascript Are Set to Run in Your Browser. Many of the Web sites in this book, especially the coloring book ones, require that your browser is capable of and set to run Java and/or JavaScript (the latter is a related language created by Netscape). Java is a Web-based scripting language that is often required to run animation or interact with a Web site. You'll need an up-to-date browser; the oldies don't support Java. If you're running Netscape select Preferences from the Edit menu. In the pop-up dialogue box click on the Advanced category to expand it. Place checks beside Enable Java and Enable JavaScript. Then click OK.

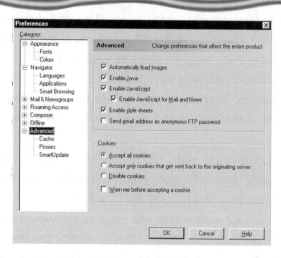

If you're browsing with Internet Explorer, select Internet Options from the Tools menu. Head to the Security tab. Click the Internet icon and click the Custom Level button. In the pop-up Security Settings box that appears, place a check besides Run ActiveX Controls and Plugins. ActiveX is Microsoft's answer to Java. It's not found on a lot of Web sites, but it does appear on many Microsoft "channels" and related sites. Under the Java category, enable the Java scripting features, and put it on Medium or High Safety. If you set it to High Safety, Explorer will prompt you before running any Java script.

How safe is Java? Can a Java script contain a virus or anything that could damage your system? While anything is possible in computers, the actual likelihood of this is extremely slim. Java applets are confined to running in a "sandbox" which is a protected area of your computer's memory, and which prevents them from interfering with other applications, files, or system resources. You can read more about Java security at the Web site of maker Sun (**http://wwwjava.sun.com/sfaq**). But our advice is to enable Java in your browser and don't lose sleep over it.

◎ PLUG-IN TROUBLESHOOTING

Step 1. Say you've logged into a Web site that you know plays music, but your browser is eerily quiet. Assuming you've heard music come from your computer before, and you know it's set up properly to play it, what should you do? First, make sure the volume is turned up. If you're running Windows 95/98 there should be a volume icon in the tray at the bottom of your screen. Click on it to get a pop-up box to adjust the sound. If you're using a Mac go to the Control Panels under your Apple menu and select Monitor and Sounds. After clicking Sounds, be sure the volume is up and the Mute button is not checked.

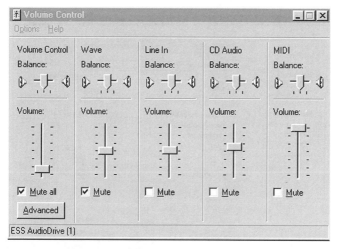

If your PC can't play sound it may be because someone set the Mute All feature to stifle the annoying whooshes and chirps of Windows' desktop themes as the user opens and closes windows.

Step 2. If you're running Windows 95/98 click the Start button and head to Settings/Control Panel, click the Internet Icon and head to the Advanced tab. Scroll down to Multimedia and place checks beside Show pictures, Play animations, Play videos, and Play sounds. Click OK to make the changes permanent.

Step 3. If you know what kind of music file it is that the Web site you're visiting is trying to send you—some Web pages tell you, on others you can find out by selecting View/Page Source then sifting through the Web page code—a feat only for the ambitious—you can determine how your PC is set up to handle it. Click the Start button, head to Settings/Folders and Icons, then click to the File Types tab. In Netscape, head to Edit/Preferences and in the dialog box expand Navigator. Then head to Applications, as shown in the above figure. You can scroll down the list of file types and see in the box at the bottom of the screen what plug-in or application, if any, is set up to play a particular sort of file.

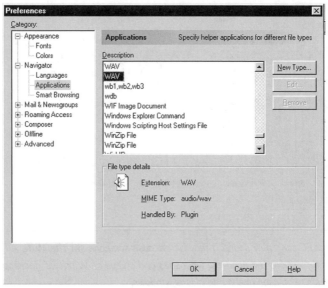

You can check how your Windows 95/98 computer handles specific file types by heading to this informative box. But whatever you do, don't click that Edit button! That is a dangerous button. You can completely confuse your computer by messing with this. Judy did this once, and had to spend four hours on the phone with Microsoft tech support to resurrect her PC. The entire time the techs clucked, "Lady, this has got to be the stupidest thing we've ever heard of anyone doing to their PC." But after writing about it in a magazine, she heard from hundreds of people who had confused their systems in the very same way. Don't you do it too!

Step 4. You can also see what plug-ins are installed in Netscape 4.0 by typing About Plug-ins in the address bar or by pulling down the Help menu and selecting About Plug-ins. (Mac users can do this too.) This menu is only moderately informative however. There is no similar feature in Internet Explorer.

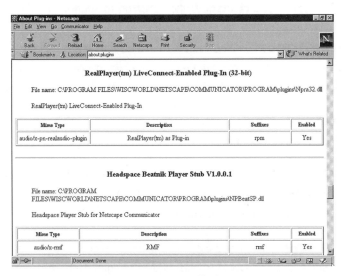

You can find out what plug-ins are installed in Netscape by typing About Plug-ins in the location bar.

Step 5. If you're running Internet Explorer the browser must be set to run plug-ins. To check on this setting, pull down the View menu and select Internet Options if you're running an older version of Explorer. Or, in newer versions, head to the Tools menu and select Internet Options. Head to the Security tab. With Internet Zone selected, place a check beside the Custom settings and click the Settings button. Or click the Custom Level button. Scroll down through the security settings and make sure that Run Active-X Control and Plug-ins is enabled.

◎ DOWNLOADING AND INSTALLING PLUG-INS

Now you should know for certain whether your browser is set up to play music. If it still can't, you may need to download and install a plug-in or two. Here are the indispensables ones for viewing movies and animation, and listening to sound:

Adobe Acrobat — You'll need this free document reader from Adobe (**http://www.adobe.com**) in order to display coloring book pages on some Web sites, as well as other art documents.

RealPlayer — It plays sound, video, and animation (**http://www.realaudio.com**).

QuickTime — You'll need this video viewer from Apple to view movies on the Web that are stored in the QuickTime format (**http://www.apple.com/quicktime**).

Shockwave — You need Shockwave to "interact" with some Web sites, such as Disney's and enjoy the animation (**http://www.macromedia.com**). You also need Shockwave to color on some of the Web-based coloring books.

Cosmo Player — You'll need Cosmo Player to play games and enjoy 3D animation on some Web sites (**http://cosmosoftware.com**).

Test your browser's sound and animation capabilities by heading to HamsterDance (**http://www.hamsterdance.com**). Gather the kids around the computer, crank up the volume, and sing along!

◎ MAKING THE INTERNET SAFE FOR YOUR KIDS—AND FOR YOURSELF

The Web is like any other public place in that if your children are young, you need to guide them. But you need to keep yourself safe too. Here are our tips:

First, sit down with your family and create an "**Internet Family Privacy Plan**." Draft these rules:

- No one will put any personal information such as their name, address, phone number, or information about siblings in e-mail, or share it in a chat room or bulletin board.

- No one will share any photos of themselves or family members with others online.

- No one will tell anyone their online password, even if they receive a message from someone claiming to work for America Online or the Internet service.

- No one will respond to any sales pitches online.

- No one will answer e-mail from strangers.

- No one will fill out any questionnaires; game or contest entry forms, or surveys on a Web site without asking for parental permission. Many Web sites gather e-mail addresses through innocuous looking surveys. All you need do is check an answer box to some question like "Do you like rock n' roll?" and hit the "submit" button and the site has your e-mail address.

- No one will type mom or dad's credit card number into an online service or commercial Web site.

- No one will arrange to meet strangers they befriend online.

Some children's Web sites ask that children enter private information about themselves before they can access the site. This is certainly to ensure that it is really children who are using the messaging features of the site. But it's also for marketing purposes. In fact, there's one well-known encyclopedia available online that asks some rather probing questions before giving kids access.

When we asked their PR firm why, they claimed it was to tailor Web pages to the individual child's needs, but when pressed, they admitted it was really for their marketing department.

Teach your children to ask you before entering any information about themselves into these sites, even their names. Look for the Trustee seal on the site (**http://www.etrust.com**). This means that the site has worked with the Trustee non-profit group to draft a policy on how they're using private information and has agreed to be monitored by Trustee. If there's no Trustee seal, look for a statement of the site's privacy policy.

Talk to your kids regularly about the Web sites they're visiting, and remind them of the need for caution when communicating with others online. Ask them to tell you about any e-mail that makes them feel uncomfortable. People are not always who they seem online. Someone who claims to be another teenager in a chat room could turn out to be a masher. If your kids insist on meeting someone they've corresponded with online in person, make them promise to take you along, and insist that the meeting be in a public place.

Often kids know more about the Internet than their parents do. Turn the tables and make sure you know at least as much as your kids. Better, spend time with your kids on the computer. Make Web surfing an activity you do together.

Some parents keep the computer out of the bedroom and place it instead in the family room or other "public" place in the house where they can work with their kids.

When you shop for an Internet service provider look for one that will block access to objectionable Web sites. Consider purchasing browser-filtering software like CyberPatrol (**http://www.cyberpatrol.com**) or Net Nanny (**http://www.netnanny.com**). These programs aren't foolproof— clever kids can deactivate them, but they're still worthwhile. Set them up to block your child's access to newsgroups and chat rooms.

If you're on America Online, familiarize yourself with the service's privacy and protection features. (See "Keeping Kids Safe on America Online", page 33). Ask the service to put a cap on your monthly bill, so the kids don't run it up to astronomical proportions.

If you plan to participate in public discussion groups use a separate Internet account or e-mail address. America Online's software permits one to set up five password-protected screen names for each household. Some Internet services will provide multiple e-mail addresses for a single account. Since spammers collect e-mail addresses by sifting through public message groups this will help keep the flood of unwanted solicitations out of the family's e-mail box.

If you think that someone is stalking your child online, do contact local police and the online service or your Internet provider and ask for help.

If you have teenagers, make sure they don't spend excessive amounts of time in chat rooms. Keep watch for unusually high phone bills. And talk to them about the time they spend online—not judgmentally, but as a concerned friend.

Visit These Web Sites for More Kid Safety Advice

SAFEKIDS.COM
http://www.safekids.com

TEEN SAFETY ONLINE
http://www.safeteens.com

SESAME STREET PARENTS
http://www.ctw.org/parents/index.cgi?ford/

THE FBI'S SAFETY TIPS FOR KIDS
http://www.fbi.gov/kids/internet/internet.htm

Visit the Consumer Product Safety Commission's Web Site for More Kid SafetyAdvice You'll find a library of articles at the cyber-home of the Consumer Product Safety Commission **(http://www.cpsc.gov/cpscpub/pubs/chld_sfy.html)**, on how to make your home safe for kids, how to buy products that are safe for children, and how to keep your kids safe.

⦿ KEEPING KIDS SAFE ON AMERICA ONLINE

America Online has been alert to parents' concerns about child safety on the service, and offers a number of features to customize your child's use of the service as well as keep offensive material out of his or her mailbox. Parents can block kids' access to chat rooms, Internet newsgroups, and block unsavory mail. While these features are nice, they shouldn't be a substitute for talking to your child and following the precautions listed in previous pages.

How to Find the Parental Controls Click the My AOL button and select Parental Controls from the drop-down menu.

What They Are: America Online lets you set up multiple passwords—protected "screen names" for your household. You can set one up for each child, and, using your master password, give the account Kids Only access (that means no Instant Messages, the child can't enter chat rooms, they cannot receive mail containing pictures, and they can access only Web sites approved for their age group); Young Teen Access (the child can enter chat rooms but only public ones monitored by AOL, they can only visit Web sites approved for their age group); or Mature Teen (the child has more access to the Internet).

How to Customize Your Child's AOL Access Say you want your child to receive e-mail only from designated addresses, or you want to give them the ability to access Internet newsgroups but not ones in which raunchy material may be contained. Click on Custom Controls to tailor the service to your child.

How to Customize Your Child's AOL Instant Messenger Access Instant Messenger is a nifty way to chat with your friends while they are online. It's similar to e-mail, except your sent message immediately appears on the recipient's computer monitor. Although AOL offers this service, AOL offers it to anyone with Internet access. Information on how to use Instant Messenger and set up your Buddy List is under AOL Keyword "Instant Messenger" or from AOL's web page (http://www.aol.com). The problem with Instant Messages is they can be disruptive and you can get unwanted messages from strangers. To customize Instant Messenger, click on Setup from the bottom of the AOL Instant Messenger box. Then select Controls from the left column. In this area you can insert the names of those you want to exchange messages with or block messages altogether.

Where to Report Problems Use the keywords Notify AOL to report any problems that you or your child encounter on the service.

America Online offers several ways parents can tailor their child's online experience to their age—and keep them safe at the same time. Use the keywords "Parental Controls" to get to them.

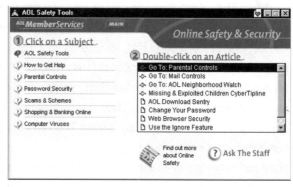

Beware of hyperlinks in e-mail sent to you by strangers & an AOL Rewards related scam.

AOL Neighborhood Watch gives you the tools and tips you need to ensure a safe and fun online experience for you and your family. Watch a quick online movie about our online safety tools, and start educating yourself today on Online Scams and Schemes in Suggested Safeguards.

Notify AOL   **Shopping & Banking**

Parental Controls: Take charge of your kids' online experience.

E-mail Safety: Find out what you can do about junk mail and more.

Computer Viruses: Protect your computer against damaging viruses.

Suggested Safeguards: Tips to keep your online time fun and safe.

Keyword: Neighborhood Watch

Use the key-words "neigh-borhood watch" to tap into a public forum and more informa-tion on keeping your child safe on AOL.

◎ WEB BROWSERS OFFER WEB SITE SCREENING, BUT KID SCREENING SOFTWARE IS STILL BEST

Netscape and Internet Explorer both offer features that will block your kids from Web sites with violence, nudity, and bad language. But the browsers rely on the Web sites' voluntarily agreeing to be screened according to guidelines set by screening organizations. Needless to say, not all raunchy Web sites agree to participate in this screening. What's more these features may block you and your child from visiting decent Web sites whose only fault is not having registered with the screening service. Software like Cyber Patrol and Net Nanny, which actually screen Web sites themselves, still provide a far more effective means of keeping bad things from young eyes.

You should still give these features in your browser a try—particularly the Content Advisor feature in Internet Explorer, which you can tailor to your child's age. From Explorer's Tools menu select Internet Options. Head to the Content tab and click the Enable button under Content Advisor. You can tailor the levels of bad language, nudity, and violence that your child sees on the Web. You can also select from several content screening agencies, such as the Recreational Software Advisory Council or RASCi (**http://www.rsac. org/ratingsv01.html**). Be sure to read the settings carefully. (In the case of RSACi the Web sites actually rate themselves.)

In Netscape 4.0 or later, go online, and from the browser's Help menu select Netwatch. It will guide you through the set-up to create password-protected content screening along the guidelines of PICS, the Platform for Internet Content Selection. But again, Web sites' participation in the PICS program is voluntary.

If You Use Your Browser's Content Screening Feature, Remember the Passsword!

Every so often someone e-mails us to say that they set up the Web site screening feature in their browser, forgot the password, and now can't visit any other Web sites besides ones for children. Don't let this happen to you! Keep the password in your safe deposit box if you must. Yes, there are ways to resurrect your browser but since this is a book for kids we're not going to reveal them.

Keep Your Browser Current to Keep Your Computer Secure

Hardly a month goes by without someone finding a new security hole in a popular browser—and its maker quickly plugging it. Keep your Web browser current—and your e-mail software too, by visiting the Web sites of their makers regularly and downloading any security patches or new versions. Be sure you download those only from their makers' Web sites. There have been reports of people receiving via e-mail "security patches" for Microsoft products that were actually hacker code to steal passwords.

⊙ WILL MY COMPUTER CATCH A VIRUS?

Viruses are noxious bits of program code that travel in computer files—usually program files—and plant themselves on your disk for the purpose of wreaking havoc.

The best way to avoid contracting a virus is to scan any program that you download from the Internet with a virus-checker, prior to running it. Our favorite is the $50 Norton AntiVirus from Symantec (**http://www.symantec.com**, 800/441-7234, 541/334-6054). Be sure to keep its virus database updated by downloading monthly upgrades from Symantec's Web site.

You should also scan any disk or CD-ROM of software that you buy, prior to installing it. Several viruses have been spread through commercially distributed software.

You should be especially careful to scan any disks or CD-ROMs that have been in your work computer, or come from the computers of your child's friends.

You should not open any file attachment that comes with an e-mail message from a stranger. Delete it, and if it was ever dangerous, your computer will never know.

Your Computer Cannot Contract a Virus by Your Tapping into a Web Site or Reading an E-mail Message. Passing disks between work, school, and home computers, and opening e-mail attachments from strangers, is the most common way in which viruses are spread.

◎ WEB SEARCHERS THAT ARE SAFE FOR KIDS TO USE

Type "Barney" into your typical Web searcher and chances are slim that the "hits" or Web pages that the searcher comes up will have anything to do with the Big Purple One. In fact, they'll probably range in topic from "Barney Frank" to raunchy renditions of the Barney song. Hardly stuff for young eyes. Here are some Web searchers that screen the Web sites they list in answer to a search.

As a parent you should carefully read the descriptions of how they screen sites. For instance, do they screen just a listed Web site, or do they screen one or more levels of links that are included in that site? And what are their criteria for screening children's sites?

These searchers also serve different purposes. Kids Click, for example, is a searcher in which Web sites are screened by librarians. Ask Jeeves, on the other hand, isn't exactly a searcher, but rather kids type their questions and the service comes up with some sort of answer culled from Web sites. Ask Eric is similarly a homework helper.

AOL NET FIND FOR KIDS ONLY
http://www.aol.com/netfind/kids/

KIDS CLICK: SEARCH ENGINE FOR KIDS
http://sunsite.berkeley.edu/KidsClick!/

KIDS TOOLS FOR SEARCHING THE INTERNET
http://www.rcls.org/ksearch.htm

ONE KEY: KIDS SAFE SEARCH ENGINE
http://www.onekey.com/live/sourc01.htm

ASK JEEVES FOR KIDS
http://www.ajkids.com/

ASK ERIC
http://ericir.syr.edu/Virtual/

Use the bookmark tips on pages 16-17
to create custom search buttons or folders for
kids in your browser.

free Big Arts and Craft Sites for the Whole Family

Whether you're an eight-year-old searching for a way to make elves out of beads and popcorn or a septuagenarian ready to take the bold step into knotting macramé, you'll find hours worth of inspiration at these Web sites. Many are assembled by craft and family magazines. Craft store chains host some. All offer lots of craft project ideas, instructions, and advice. One can easily spend an entire evening surfing these "virtual craft magazines."

⭐ Family Magazines that Offer Free Craft Project Instructions

BETTER HOMES AND GARDENS CRAFTS PAGE
http://www.bhglive.com/food/crafts/craftdex.htm
Better Homes & Gardens *offers craft projects especially for kids, such as making lace heart baskets and silly glasses. Adults will also find directions for decorative crafts such as leaf topiary and wheat garlands.*

FAMILY.COM

http://family.go.com

In this cyber-magazine for families, sponsored by Disney, you'll find lots of activities to keep the kids busy, such as "making stuff with newspapers," plus good reading for mom and dad too.

FAMILYFUN MAGAZINE

http://www.familyfun.com

Directions for tinfoil-paper, juice-can puppets, and "rain painting" are among the projects you'll find at this wonderful site hosted by the magazine.

PARENTS MAGAZINE

http://www.parentsmagazine.com

Parents Magazine *offers an "activity finder" that lets you select the age group and activity (like crafts). The Web site will produce a list of hundreds of projects applicable to that age group.*

SCHOLASTIC'S PARENT AND CHILD

http://www.scholastic.com/parentandchild

The magazine offers a guide to "family activities" for newborns to age 6.

WOMEN'S DAY ONLINE

On America Online use the keywords "women's day."
If you're on America Online you can tap into the Women's Day *forum, which offers a large selection of craft projects and advice for all ages.*

Big Web Sites for Big Craft Stores Where You'll Find Free Project Instructions

Do memories of your childhood include stealing away with a quarter to pedal to the Ben Franklin store? You no longer need to ride your bike across town to get to your favorite craft store. Just tap into its Web site for inspiration, craft instruction sheets, and product ideas.

A.C. MOORE
http://www.acmoore.com

BEN FRANKLIN CRAFTS
http://www.bfranklincrafts.com
http://www.bfranklincrafts.com/kid.htp

BEVERLY'S ONLINE: KIDS CRAFTS ROOM
http://beverlys.com/kids.htm

ENTERPRISE ART
http://www.enterpriseart.com/index.html

JO-ANN FABRICS AND CRAFTS
http://www.joann.com

MICHAELS ARTS AND CRAFTS
http://www.michaels.com

MJ DESIGNS — THE CREATIVITY STORE
http://www.mjdesigns.com

 Big Craft Web Sites with Craft How-Tos and Discussions

ARTS AND CRAFTS FROM DELPHI
http://www.delphi.com/crafts/masterindex1.html
You'll find articles on basket making, beading, dollmaking, glass etching, holiday crafts, and more at this incredible site.

101 ACTIVITIES TO DO WITH YOUR TODDLER
http://www.personal.engin.umich.edu/~ajdrake/toddler/open.htm
Julie Drake offers ideas on crafts for toddlers that were e-mailed to her by parents from around the world. You'll also find songs and finger plays.

AUNT ANNIE'S CRAFTS
http://www.auntannie.com
You'll find over 225 craft projects, most for kids, at Aunt Annie's. New projects are added weekly.

BLUEBONNET VILLAGE CRAFT NETWORK

http://www.bluebonnetvillage.com/

You'll find craft instructions, project ideas, and lists of suppliers courtesy of Nora Creeach.

CRAFT IDEAS

http://www.nectar.com.au/~jascraig/craft

Jacinta Thomler offers a directory of craft projects compiled from various Internet discussion groups. Projects include holiday crafts, paper crafts, and crafts for kids.

Web page created by Jacinta Thomler

CRAFT PALS BULLETIN BOARD

http://www.craftpals.org/bbs1/index.html

Craft Pals offers discussion groups for many different kinds of crafts, plus special discussion areas for kids and moms.

CRAFTNET VILLAGE

http://www.craftnetvillage.com

You'll find a database of craft projects, a crafter's bulletin board, and more.

CRAFTERS UNITE
http://web.kilroys.net/~rosimons
You'll find craft projects, links, craft chats, swaps.

THE CRAFTER'S COMMUNITY
http://www.crafterscommunity.com
You'll find craft pen pals, projects, discussion groups, and a craft-related Web ring at this site.

CYBERCAMP
http://cybercamp.unl.edu
You'll find camp games and crafts at this site run by the U.S. Department of Agriculture.

DISNEY
http://www.disney.go.com
The Walt Disney Web site is always a great spot to visit for crafts—as well as games and other fun.

FISKARS CRAFT PROJECTS
http://www.fiskars.com/crafts/craft_projects/craft_projects.html
Fiskars offers a world of possibilities on things you can make with scissors. (We bet Edward Scissorhands visits often.)

FAMILIES UNITED ON THE NET

http://www.thefunplace.com

This affiliate of cyber toystore eToys offers craft discussion boards, project ideas, recipes, and more.

THE GREAT CRAFTS IDEA PAGE

http://CraftPage.WebRequests.com

You'll find project instructions, free offers, and links to kids crafting projects.

I CAN MAKE THIS WITH STYROFOAM!

http://www.styrofoam-crafts.com/projects/index.htm

Of course you can! When we were in grade school we even made a moon rover out of Styrofoam (take that NASA!). You'll find hundreds of craft ideas at the cyber-home of the makers of every six-year-old's favorite building material, including directions on how to make barnyard animals and dinosaurs.

I CRAFT

http://www.i-craft.com

The Hobby Industry Association runs this great site where you'll find crafting tips, lessons, and a regularly changing roster of projects such as the yo-yo wreath, stenciled boxes, a memory album, a lampshade, and a craft pack.

🛒 JANA'S CRAFT CONNECTION

http://www.wyomingcompanion.com/janacraft/index.htm

Jana Gallagher's site offers help for crafty folks and craft projects for both older kids and preschoolers.

® 1999 Jana Gallagher

JEAN AND JULIE'S CRAFT CLUB PROJECT INDEX

http://web.craftnet.org/c90/jeanjule/projects.htm

Jean Kievlan and Julie McGuffee share a large selection of craft projects.

LINIT STARCH-N-CRAFTS IDEA SITE

http://www.linit.com

Where would crafts be without starch? Our crocheted snowflakes would be limp. Our cheesecloth ghosts would lack their eerie brittleness. The folks at Linit offer ideas for crafting as well as decorating (decorating with starch? it can be done). And of course they provide lots of ways that you can use gallons of starch in your projects.

MAKE STUFF.COM
http://www.makestuff.com
"Remember, its not home-made—it's hand-crafted" is the motto of this vast site, which offers directions on how to make just about anything.

CRAFTS FOR KIDS AT ABOUT.COM
http://craftsforkids.about.com
You'll find hundreds of craft project how-tos here, plus links to more information around the Web, on just about every kid-craft imaginable, from making stuff with putty to making stuff with buttons.

WENDY'S WORLD OF CRAFTS AND FUN
http://www.netfix.com/poptart/master.htm
Wendy Hogan offers craft projects for all the different holidays. She also provides an excellent list of links to Web sites for children and parents.

 ## Web Sites of Craft Industry Magazines

CRAFTS'N THINGS ONLINE
http://www.craftsnthings.com

THE CRAFTS REPORT ONLINE
http://www.craftsreport.com

THE GREAT CRAFT IDEAS PAGE
http://CraftPage.WebRequests.com

TIP

Head to a Web-based Bulletin Board to Talk Crafts

Looking for other rubber stampers to talk to? How about fans of making paper dragons? The chances are that no matter how obscure your favorite craft is, there's a discussion group for it somewhere in cyberspace. Judith Perry of Dragon Web Works has compiled a list of craft-talk bulletin boards. Most are for stamping, paper crafts, and scrapbook making (**http://www.littlebit.com/rs_bb.htm**). You'll also find craft zealots talking it up in the Web Craft Forum Exchange (**http://www.craftweb.com/bbs/www board.htm**).

more free
Collections of
Kids' Craft
Project Instructions

"I am constantly searching for things to keep my little ones busy," writes Lisa, a full-time mother of five. "I figure there are a lots of others who are looking for the same thing. That's why I decided to create this site." Her Web site Arts-N-Craft by Lisa (http:www.inmotion-pcs.com/amass/theboss/artsn.htm) offers directions for oodles of great craft projects for kids— from egg carton flowers to potpourri teddybears and a matchbox sewing kit. You'll find many other parents and teachers who've created similar sites on the web. They're great repositories of ideas to keep little hands (and big ones) busy on a rainy day.

BIG TOP PRODUCTIONS' ARTS AND CRAFTS
http://www.bigtop.com/kids/crafts_1110.html
Learn how to make candleholders out of tin cans, Guatemalan "worry dolls," and scented frames.

CRAFTPALS BY COTTAGE CRAFTS
http://craftpals.org/directory.html
A Fourth of July windsock, paper mache recipes, sculpting dough, and camp ideas are some of the projects you'll find at this site.

CRAYOLA CRAFT CENTRAL
http://www.crayola.com/craft_index.html
From the makers of Crayola comes a site devoted to all the clever things you can do with crayons—from making prints to planters to puppets.

THE FAMILY EDUCATION NETWORK

http://www.FamilyEducation.com/

This huge Web site for families offers news and features on many topics of interest to parents and kids. They offer free craft tutorials—select an age group, head to Activities and click Crafts.

CULTURE QUEST WORLD TOUR

http://www.ipl.org/youth/cquest

Join Olivia Owl and Parsifal Penguin on their tour around the world. Watch them play the games, see the museums full of arts and crafts, listen to folktales, and learn about the holidays, crafts, and festivals of many of the world's cultures.

🛒 DINOSAURS, DINOSAURS, AND MORE DINOSAURS!

http://www.dinodon.com

Don Lessem and Dinosaur Productions present a page full of dinosaurs, including a dino dictionary, a weekly quiz, and dinosaur links.

"EARLY CHILDHOOD ARTS AND CRAFTS" BY SCHOOL DISCOUNT SUPPLY

http://www.earlychildhood.com/art.html

You'll find new project instructions each month.

Visit the About.com's Kids Exchange for Craft How-Tos You'll find a whole bunch of craft projects and ideas, from making Easter bunnies to mastering the art of tie-dyeing at About.com's Kids Exchange (**http://kidexchange. about.com**) run by Wendy Hogan. You need to do some searching on the site to find the craft stuff—head to the library, and search past articles.

ENCHANTED LEARNING SOFTWARE'S KINDERCRAFTS

http://www.EnchantedLearning.com/crafts

You'll find a wide selection of free project instructions for kids in preschool, kindergarten, and elementary school.

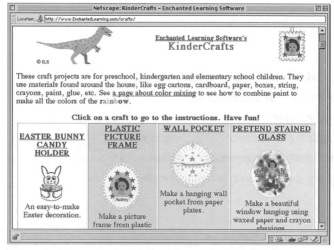

Netscape: KinderCrafts – Enchanted Learning Software

Location: http://www.EnchantedLearning.com/crafts/

Enchanted Learning Software's
KinderCrafts

© ELS

These craft projects are for preschool, kindergarten and elementary school children. They use materials found around the house, like egg cartons, cardboard, paper, boxes, string, crayons, paint, glue, etc. See a page about color mixing to see how to combine paint to make all the colors of the rainbow.

Click on a craft to go to the instructions. Have fun!

EASTER BUNNY CANDY HOLDER	PLASTIC PICTURE FRAME	WALL POCKET	PRETEND STAINED GLASS
An easy-to-make Easter decoration.	Make a picture frame from plastic	Make a hanging wall pocket from paper plates.	Make a beautiful window hanging using waxed paper and crayon shavings

© 1999 Enchanted Learning.com

FREEBIES FROM KIDS CRAFT BASE

http://www.vistek.com/html/kidcraft.html

Kids Craft Base offers a free monthly project or pattern you can print. Past projects include a birdfeeder, lace ornaments, and T-shirt pillows.

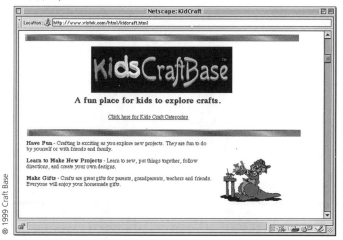

FUN CRAFTS FOR KIDS

http://tac.shopnetmall.com/www.funroom.com/CraftIndex.html

Topics to keep you busy include bubbles, gooey stuff, chalk, paper mache, and colored sand.

FUN THINGS FOR KIDS TO DO

http://www.ozemail.com.au/~wprimary/acts.htm

This Australian site includes instructions for making a hopping kangaroo and other Down Under wonders.

THE IDEA BOX

http://www.theideabox.com

You'll find directions to make a crayon melt picture, bean bunnies, button rings, kazoos, and more. Also games and songs.

JUST 4 GIRLS

http://www.girlscouts.org/girls

Check out the Girls Ask How feature on this site from the Girl Scouts. On the Making Stuff pages you'll find directions for projects like a decoupage box.

 ## KIDS CRAFT BULLETIN BOARD

http://www.wwvisions.com/craftbb/kids.html

Moms and Dads can exchange messages about the troubles and toils of kid crafts.

 ## BUSY HANDS CRAFT SUPPLIES' KIDS PROJECTS

http://www.utec.net/bhcs/kids.htm

You'll learn everything you ever wanted to know about salt dough, finger puppets, string art, and making macaroni box purses at this colorful site.

 ## MAKINGFRIENDS.COM: CRAFTS FOR KIDS

http://makingfriends.com/index.htm

THE YUCKY STUFF PAGE

http://www.makingfriends.com/yucky.htm

You'll find directions for hundreds of free craft projects including beading and preschool jewelry-making. Be sure to visit The Yucky Stuff Page for "projects so gross that even kids who hate crafts will love them." Examples: "squished bugs" and "bagged heads."

RAINY DAY RESOURCE PAGE

http://www.cp.duluth.mn.us/~sarah

You'll find projects involving bubbles, finger paint, and more at this online guide to activities for children.

SQUIGLY'S PLAYHOUSE

http://www.SquiglysPlayhouse.com

Follow the arts and crafts link in Barb Willner's playhouse for instructions on making a paper mache piggy bank or marbleized stationery. You'll also find pages to color.

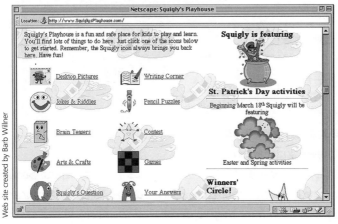

SUMMER FUN

http://db.ok.bc.ca/summer

If you think there's nothing to do, check out this site full of activities.

Visit Jell-O's Web Site for Crafts You Can Eat Ever since they started making blue Jell-O we began to wonder whether Jell-O wasn't for crafting as much as for eating. At the Web home of Jell-O (**http://ww.jello.com**) you'll find recipes for things you never thought possible, such as gelatin Easter eggs. And who can resist Jigglers? Best of all, if your project doesn't look good, you can always eat it.

⭐ Help Other Kids—Through Crafts

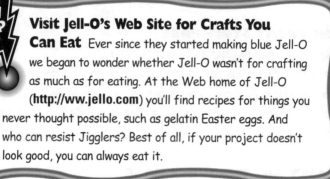

KIDS CARE CLUBS

http://www.kidscare.org

Kids Care Clubs are clubs formed by kids to help others. Some Kids Care projects include collecting hats for kids with cancer (many kids send hats they've decorated themselves) and assembling decorated "hope chests" for needy kids. Learn how you can get involved at the Kids Care Web site.

CHILDREN'S HOSPITAL OF PHILADELPHIA ART GALLERY

http://www.oncolink.com/images/child/gallery3.html

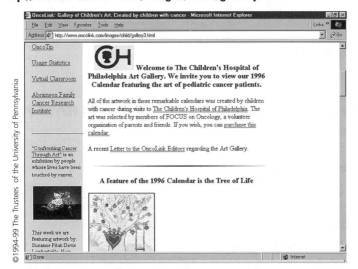

*At the University of Pennsylvania's Oncolink (**http://www.oncolink.com**) you'll find an online gallery of art by children combating cancer. Stop by and write a note of hope, and read what other kids have to say about cancer.*

There are many other Web sites where kids can learn about volunteer projects, and get involved. A good place to start is Are You Into It? (**http://areyouintoit.com**). Stop by the Peace Corps Kids World (**http://www.peacecorps.gov/kids**) to learn how the Peace Corps is making a difference in other kids' lives.

Visit Other Just-for-Kids Web Sites for More Fun

There are lots of great Web sites just for kids. Here are some of our favorites. Many offer songs and games, plus "online activity pages."

CYBERKIDS
http://www.cyberkids.com/

KIDSCOM: PLAY SMART, STAY SAFE, AND HAVE FUN
http://www.kidscom.com/

KIDS DOMAIN
http://www.kidsdomain.com/

KIDIDDLES
http://www.kididdles.com/

At KIDiddles, MoJo's Musical Mouseum offers a database of lyrics to favorite kid's songs, you'll find games for kids, and a never-ending story that kids can write episodes for.

KIDS SPACE
http://www.kids-space.org/

KIDS OF THE WEB
http://www.wenet.net/~leroyc/kidsweb/

KID WORLD, BY KIDS FOR KIDS

http://www.bconnex.net/~kidworld/

LOOK, LEARN & DO

http://www.looklearnanddo.com/

Tap into craft project instructions, games, coloring pages, and
links to libraries, encyclopedias, and home schooling resources at
Look, Learn & Do.

Web Sites Where You'll Find Recipes for Dough, Paint, and Other Goopy Stuff

Looking for a recipe for faux Playdough? How about body paint? Or maybe you're looking for a recipe for bubble-blowing solution. You'll find them on these Web sites:

CRAFT RECIPES

http://www.melborponsti.com/speirs/crafts/index.htm
http://ucunix.san.uc.edu/~edavis/kids-list/crafts/doughs.html
Recipes for sculpting dough, putty, paint, and more, compiled by Ellen Davis.

CRAFTPALS BY COTTAGE CRAFTS

http://craftpals.org/directory.html

DIANE BUNDY'S RECIPES FOR CRAFT DOUGHS, PAINT, AND GOO

http://www.ptialaska.net/~bundyd/paper.html

free Coloring Pages and Craft How-Tos from the Web Sites of TV Shows and Cartoons

Almost every TV show and entertainment network has a Web site. We've culled through them and selected those that offer features to help kids exercise their creativity. The Web sites for PBS shows (**http://www.pbs.org/kids**) are especially wonderful places to look for coloring pages and craft activity ideas. The first half of this chapter lists Web sites that offer coloring pages for kids to print and crayon. At the end of the chapter you'll find a list of Web sites for TV shows devoted to crafts. We've divided them into shows for kids and shows for adults.

Note: *You may wonder why we haven't included Web sites of many other popular kids' shows in this chapter. We've listed only those that offer coloring pages or other craft activities.*

Web Sites for TV Shows that Offer Coloring Pages and Craft Projects for Tikes

Many of these Web sites offer not only coloring pages, but animations, games, and sound you can enjoy with your child

BARNEY

Barney has two online homes—at Barney Online and at PBS. You'll find coloring pages at both.

- BARNEY ONLINE
  http://barneyonline.com/Barney/Nav/home.html

- BARNEY AND FRIENDS
  http://www.pbs.org/barney

SESAME STREET AND THE MUPPETS

The Muppets sing and play on several Web sites. In addition to the sites listed below you'll also find them making appearances on Disney's site (**http://www.disney.com**).

- THE CHILDREN'S TELEVISION WORKSHOP FAMILY WORKSHOP
  http://www2.ctw.org
  http://www2.ctw.org/celebrate/athome

- MUPPETS AT HOME
  http://www.muppets.com

- SESAME STREET
  http://www.pbs.org/kids/sesame

- THE JIM HENSON CO.
  http://www.henson.com

TELETUBBIES

- TELETUBBIES ON PBS
  http://www.pbs.org/teletubbies

- BBC ONLINE EDUCATION: TELETUBBIES
  http://www.bbc.co.uk/education/teletubbies

THEODORE TUGBOAT

- THEODORE TUGBOAT
  http://www.cochran.com/theodore/activities

- THEODORE TUGBOAT AT PBS
  http://www.pbs.org/tugboat

PBS KIDS

http://www.pbs.org/kids
Here's where you'll find the cyberhomes of the Teletubbies, Arthur, Charlie Horse, Kratts' Creatures, Mr. Rogers, Noddy, Storytime, Barney, Theodore Tugboat, Totts TV, Wimzie's House, ZOOm , and Zoboomafoo. Also there's a special area for pre-schoolers. Of special interest are the PBS Web sites below:

- ARTHUR
  http://www.pbs.org/wgbh/arthur

- MISTER ROGERS' NEIGHBORHOOD
  http://www.pbs.org/rogers

- THE MAGIC SCHOOL BUS
  http://scholastic.com/MagicSchoolBus

- PAPPYLAND
  http://www.pappyland.com

Web Sites for Book and Cartoon Characters that Offer Coloring Pages

These cyber-homes of your favorite comic characters all offer coloring pages to print and color. Many also offer free screen savers, icons, and computer backgrounds based on the character.

SEUSSVILLE
http://www.seussville.com

GARFIELD AND FRIENDS
http://www.garfield.com

SNOOPY ONLINE
http://www.unitedmedia.com/comics/peanuts

THE PEANUTS COLORING BOOK
http://www.unitedmedia.com/comics/peanuts/c_fun/html/c4.html

UNITED MEDIA'S COMICS.COM
http://www.unitedmedia.com/comics
Visit the home of the United Media Syndicate to tap into Web fun for cartoons including Frank and Ernest, For Better or Worse, Luann, Snoopy, Dilbert, and Meg.

WHERE'S WALDO
http://www.findwaldo.com

TIP

Find the Web Homes of Your Favorite Authors Head to David K. Brown's Children's Literature Web Guide (**http://www.acs.ucalgary.ca/ ~dkbrown/ index.html**) for links to Web sites of children's books—and children's books information in cyberspace. On Scholastic's Web site (**http://www.scholastic .com**) you'll find Web sites for many popular children's books, including *Goosebumps* and *The Babysitter's Club.*

 ## Web Sites for TV and Movie Networks that Offer a Bit More than Blast'em Games

All the TV and movie networks have Web sites, but these offer coloring pages related to their shows and movies. Some offer changing rosters of online crafty activities.

DISNEY
http://www.disney.com
No matter your age you'll find something fun and wondrous on the Disney Web site.

THE DISNEY CHANNEL
http://disney.go.com/DisneyChannel
Head to the Playhouse "Print It" page for coloring pages. Under "Toon Disney" you'll find more drawing fun.

FOX KIDS ONLINE
http://www.foxkids.com
Head to the animation lab to create your own cartoons online. Kids may need adult help to navigate the site.

WARNER BROTHERS KIDS PAGE

http://www.kids.warnerbros.com

Let Daffy Duck teach you to draw, build your own Scooby home page, and learn how cartoons are made. Or, head to the Coloring Corner: http://wbanimation.warnerbros.com/cmp/ani_13cc.htm

 ## Web Sites for TV Shows that Offer Craft Projects for Kids

HANDS ON: CRAFTS FOR KIDS

http://www.crafts4kids.com

DONNA'S DAY

http://www.ktca.org/donnasday

 ## Web Sites for TV Shows that Offer Craft Projects for Adults (but Kids Can Help).

THE ARTS AND CRAFTS HOUR FROM THE BBC

http://ftp.bbc.co.uk/education/hours/artcraft/index.shtml

THE CAROL DUVALL SHOW

http://www.hgtv.com

http://www.hgtv.com/carol/carol_archive_450.html

HOME AND GARDEN TELEVISION

http://www.hgtv.com/hgtv.html

The cable home to Simply Quilts, the Carol Duvall Show, and other crafty shows.

MARTHA STEWART LIVING

http://www.marthastewart.com

Tip: head to the program guide for instructions for projects seen on the TV show.

QUILTING FROM THE HEARTLAND

http://www.qheartland.com

TOWN AND COUNTRY CRAFTS WITH KATHY PETERSON

http://www.kathypeterson.com

Web Sites with free

CHAPTER 5

Coloring Pages

Y ou're never too old to color. In fact, we both keep boxes of crayons in our desk drawers and still feel a thrill at the thought of all those colors. But maybe you left your favorite coloring book at Grandma's. Maybe you left your crayons there, too. And maybe, if you're like us, that was thirty years ago. No problem. Head to the Web and print some coloring pages. If you lack crayons, some of these sites let you color online. Simply select a color on the screen and draw in color with your mouse. You may need Java or Javascript enabled in your browser for it to work, or you may need a plug-in like Shockwave. The Web site will tell you if you do. Read the directions in Chapter 1 on getting plug-ins to work (pages 22-28) if you need help.

How to Print Coloring Pages To print coloring pages use your browser's Print command in its File menu. This will print everything that's displayed on a Web page. To print just the picture, right-click on it with your mouse and from the pop-up dialog box click Save Image As... . This will save the picture to your computer's disk. You would then display it in a separate graphics program and use its File/Print command to print it. If you've already colored the page, but it doesn't print the same color as it looks on the screen, that's because sometimes colors don't translate well from screen to printer. In other words, they may look different on your computer screen than on paper.

ALEX'S BOX OF CRAYONS
http://www.kidalex.com/home.html
Patrick Jaromin and Art Today offer lots of pictures that you can color online, save or print, and even e-mail to friends.

THE CHILDREN'S BUTTERFLY SITE
http://www.mesc.usgs.gov/butterfly/Butterfly.html
Learn about butterflies and download coloring pages from this wonderful site by the U.S. Dept. of the Interior.

CIRCLE OF FRIENDS FUN PAGES
http://www.circle-of-friends.com/fun.htm
You'll find coloring pages featuring children from different lands, plus games and more.

COLORING BOOK.COM
http://www.coloringbook.com

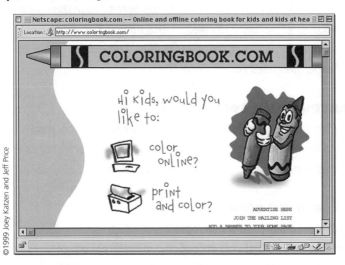

Jeff Price and Joey Katzen offer a very cool coloring book you can color online. There's even an eraser.

COLORING.COM

http://www.coloring.com

Select from holiday pictures including Halloween and football season ones, and color them with your mouse. You can even fill the pictures with patterns. When you're done, print your picture or e-mail it to a friend.

If you don't have a box of Crayola glitter crayons— get your mom or dad to buy some. They're great!

CRAYOLA

http://www.crayola.com

Call it the Mother of All Web Coloring Sites. No matter your age you'll find pictures to color at the home of crayons. Crayola's idea generator creates statements like "The robot sails in the bird cage" and asks you to draw them.

CRAYONS AND COMPUTERS

http://Members.aol.com/Sabbeth/CrayonsandComputers.html

Award-winning children's book author Carol Sabbeth shares coloring pages, crafts, and lessons about colors.

GUMBY WORLD

http://www.gumbyworld.com/colorbook

Everyone loves Gumby! Print pages depicting his adventures and color him something other than green.

THE KID'S TREEHOUSE COLORING BOOK

The Kid's Treehouse Online Community for kids offers two online coloring books, one for Java-enabled browsers, another for Shockwave users:

- THE JAVA VERSION:
  http://www.kidstreehouse.com/public/colorbk/index.html

- THE SHOCKWAVE VERSION:
  http://www.kidstreehouse.com/public/shockwave/swcolor.htm

 MICHAEL'S ELECTRIC CANVAS
http://www.michaels.com/e-canvas/e-canvas.html
An online coloring book from Michael's craft stores.

NASA'S SPACE COLORING BOOK HOME PAGE
http://tommy.jsc.nasa.gov/~woodfill/SPACEED/SEHHTML/color.html
Color pictures of the space shuttle, rockets, and other drawings from NASA.

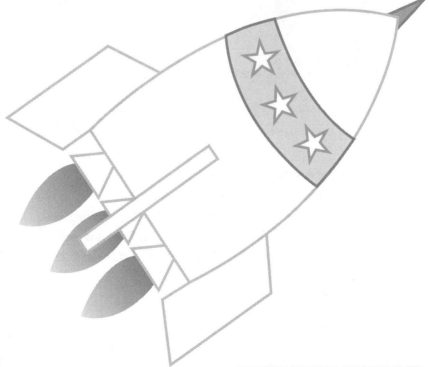

PILKEY'S WEB OF FUN

http://www.pilkey.com

Author Dav Pilkey offers coloring pages, games, puzzles, and more.

RADICALMAN

http://www.radicalman.com

You'll find an online coloring book (you'll need Shockwave to color it) and mini-posters you can print and color for your room. There are some very cool drawings from Jason McGinnis.

JAYZEEBEAR'S GREEN FOREST COLOR BOOK

http://www.jayzeebear.com/color/colorbig.html

You can color butterflies, a dinosaur, a house, and more.

Web page created by Julie Tommu. Interface graphic arts designed by Karl Hornell.

SAFETY BEAR'S COLORING BOOK

http://www.dps.state.ak.us/AST/safety/instruct.htm

The Alaska State Troopers' Crime Prevention Dept. offers coloring pictures of bears with safety messages. Print and mail your finished coloring and it could be displayed in the offices of the state troopers.

STACEY MAYER'S FREE ONLINE COLORING BOOKS

http://www.awhitehorse.com/centaur

Stacey offers wonderful line drawings of horses, unicorns, and other animals to print and color.

TOONACAT'S KIDS CLUB

http://toonacat.com

You'll find pages to color, a children's art gallery, and other fun activities like puzzles and games.

THE TRIPPYHIPPY'S COLORING BOOK

http://trippy.shano.com/colors.phtml

The TrippyHippy offers lots of great coloring book pages.

WYLAND'S WEB COLORING BOOK

http://www.wylandkids.com/9cb2_01.htm

The popular sea-life art gallery Wyland offers wonderful pictures of humpback whales, sea otters, penguins, or other marine life to print and color. The site offers information on the animals along with their picture.

WE CAN WORK IT OUT COLORING

http://members.aol.com/pforpeace/WorkItOut/color.htm

People for Peace offers an online coloring book with images of dinosaurs working out their differences.

WATER SAFETY COLORING BOOK

http://www.orn.usace.army.mil/pao/watersafety/kidspg.html

Download a 22-page water safety fun book filled with games, puzzles, and coloring pages, courtesy of Steven Foshee and the U.S. Army Corps of Engineers.

If Stains Remain after Playtime is Over, Head Over to Crayola Stain Removal Tips (http://education.crayola.com/tips/). The folks at Binney & Smith's Consumer Affairs Deparment compiled information on how to remove crayons, paints, silly putty, clay, and other products from various surfaces and fabrics.

LOOKING FOR DINOSAURS ON THE WEB?

Check out the Museum of Western Colorado
(**http://www.mwc.mus.co.us/dinosaurs**) *or the Dinosaur Link
Page* (**http://www.gla.ac.uk/~gxha14/dinol.html**).

DID ANYONE SAY "FROGS?"

Sandra Loosemore has created a Web site devoted to frogs
(**http://frog.simplenet.com/froggy/index.shtml**). *You'll find frog
information as well as frog pictures for coloring and drawing.*

CHAPTER 6
free How-Tos
for Making Stuff
with Paper

Paper, scissors, and glue are all you need to make the craft projects featured on these Web sites. Some will even show you how to make paper. Have you ever tried to quill? Quilling is the art of rolling paper and forming it into designs. It's popular in Great Britain, but you can learn it at home by visiting some of these sites. Do you have a computer printer? Then visit the Web sites devoted to computer printer crafts for ideas on making notebook covers, stickers, and more with your printer.

 Free How-Tos for Building Castles, Gas Stations, and Houses

HOW TO MAKE A CARDBOARD CASTLE
http://www.makestuff.com/cardboard_castle.html
The folks at MakeStuff.com offer instructions on fashioning your own castle.

"MAKE A TOWN" BY OWL AND MOUSE
EDUCATIONAL SOFTWARE
http://www.wolfenet.com/~por/foldup.html
Using your computer and free software you can print patterns for paper houses and stores, and then arrange them into your own town.

BEN & JERRY'S FUN STUFF

http://euphoria.benjerry.com/fun/index.html

Download and print stuff from the ice-cream makers to make your own Ben & Jerry's Gas Station. Or, print your own Ben & Jerry's cups and napkins with your computer printer. Just what you've always wanted!

HOW TO BUILD AN INEXPENSIVE PLAYHOUSE

http://members.aol.com/skygazr888/plyhs.html

Christopher Daykin explains how to build a kids playhouse with cardboard.

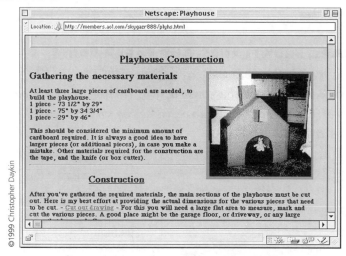

© 1999 Christopher Daykin

⭐ Free How-Tos for Making Stars, Snowflakes, and Star-like Paper Sculptures

"WOVEN PAPER STARS" BY DEANNA JOHNSON

http://www.hifiber.com/scanstar.html

Deanna Johnson and Hi Fiber Design offer directions for creating Scandinavian paper stars.

PAPER SCULPTURE FROM "GRAPHICA OBSCURA: COMPUTER GRAPHICS HACKS"

http://www.sgi.com/grafica/fold/page001.html

http://www.sgi.com/grafica/huffman/index.html

Paul Haeberli and mathematician David Huffman at the University of California, Santa Cruz explain how to create paper sculptures and stars.

SNOWFLAKES YOU CAN MAKE

http://www1.surfsouth.com/~rlogue/snowup.htm

George the Gnome explains how to fold and cut paper to create snowflakes.

STARS, SNOWFLAKES, AND PAPER BOATS

http://www.highhopes.com/maverickboats.html

Maddy and Maverick share instructions for making paper boats, plus offer links to other Web resources on making snowflakes and stars.

LEARN HOW TO MAKE A FIVE-POINTED STAR WITH ONE SNIP
http://www.libertynet.org/iha/betsy/flagstar.html
At Betsy Ross' Web page you'll learn how to create a symmetrical star. Be sure to read the pages about how the U.S. flag was designed.

 ## Free How-Tos for Making Goopy Stuff to Hold Paper Together

DIANE BUNDY'S PAPER CRAFTS
http://www.ptialaska.net/~bundyd/paper.html
Bundy offers recipes for parents and teaches paper mache, craft doughs, paint, and goo making. She also offers links to many projects that can be printed, colored, cut, and folded.

TAPPI PAPER UNIVERSITY'S ART CLASS
http://www.tappi.org/paperu/artClass/artClass.htm
Learn to make paper mache and pulp ornaments and jewelry.

Free How-Tos for Making More Amazing Things with Paper

WHAT CAN I DO WITH WALLPAPER?

http://www.angelfire.com/ia/barbspad/wallpaper.html

This is an amazing Web site. Host Barb Kay tells you how to get free wallpaper for crafts (from discarded sample books at decorating stores), how to "harvest" and store it, and how to create all sorts of stuff with it—from envelopes to gift boxes and picture frames. She offers information on the art of wallpaper crafting that she's collected from all over cyberspace.

DOWNLOAD A DINOSAUR

http://www.rain.org/~philfear/download-a-dinosaur.html

Download a triceratops, a T-rex, and other prehistoric reptiles (or mammals, for adherents of the "warm-blooded dinosaur theory"). Print them, cut them, glue them together, and turn your house into a Paleocene diorama. Courtesy of Phil Heiple and Boa Boy Productions.

Web page created by Phil Heiple

CAMMIE'S QUILLING CORNER
http://www.cjnconsulting.com/quilling/
Quilling is the art of rolling narrow strips of paper and shaping them into decorative designs. You'll find here a quilling discussion area and links to suppliers.

 ## PAPER PUPPETS AND PUPPET PATTERNS
http://www3.ns.sympatico.ca/onstage/puppets/
Learn how to make finger puppets, and read tips on making hand shadows from Stage Hand Puppets. Click on the Activity page.

CRAFTS FROM FISKARS
http://www.fiskars.com/crafts/craft_projects/craft_projects.html
Scissors-maker Fiskars offers a selection of craft how-tos for things you can make with scissors, including a "pinked Santa," greeting cards, holiday projects, and more.

ECOLAND KIDS CRAFTS
http://www.ecolad.com/just4kids/crafts.html
Learn how to make a bird feeder.

FREE BOOKMARK HOW-TOS FROM GINMEE TECH

http://www.webcom.com/gmt/freeproject.html

Ginmee offers bookmark designs and directions for making them.

 Free How-Tos for Making Paper

"HAND-MADE PAPERMAKING" BY SUE BELL, FROM DELPHI CRAFTS

http://www.delphi.com/crafts/papermake.html
http://www.delphi.com/crafts/papermak2.html
http://www.delphi.com/crafts/papermak3.html

*At the wonderful Delphi Crafts (*http://www.delphi.com/crafts*)
Web site, Bell explains in a three-part article how to create
your own paper.*

HOW TO MAKE PAPER

http://CraftPage.WebRequests.com/crafts8.htm

A nice tutorial from WebRequests.

LEARN2 MAKE PAPER

http://learn2.com/06/0697/0697.html

*The learn-how Web site Learn2.Com offers directions on making
your own paper.*

Free How-Tos for Computer Printer Crafts

HEWLETT-PACKARD'S PRINTSVILLE
http://www.hp.com/printing_ideas

HP offers lots of craft projects you can make by printing things in your computer printer. Click Kid's Clubhouse for directions on printing labels, binder covers, lunchbags, bookmarks, and more. You need the Adobe Acrobat plug-in.

"FUN WITH COLOR LASER FOIL" BY KAY HALL
http://www.c-mug.org/h/kh.Foil.html

Computer printer expert Kay Hall offers advice on nifty things you can make with laser printer foil. Check out her Web site (**http://www.printerideas.com/cpib/index.html**) *for more ideas and information on her Color Printer Idea Book which is full of kid craft projects and computer tutorials.*

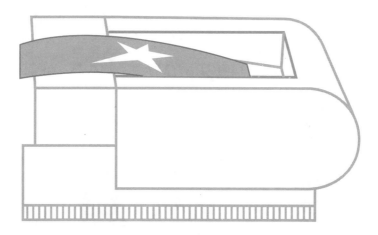

CHAPTER 7

free How-Tos
for Making
Paper Dolls
and Accessories

There is no such thing as having too many dolls. But our pocket-books may not agree. If the only surplus of paper you have is in your computer printer tray and not your wallet, head to the Web and download some dolls. You can download Shirley Temple from the home of Twentieth Century Fox. Or Florence Nightingale from the U.S. Historical Society. You'll even find Barbie—and her cute accessories—online to download and print.

🛒 PAPER DOLLS BY LUCINDA CUNNINGHAM DURBIN

http://www.paperdolls.org/index.html

The Web site of well-known doll artist Durbin offers many doll designs with clothing to print and enjoy.

©1999 Lucinda C. Durbin

THE PAPER DOLL ARCHIVE
http://www.ushsdolls.com/paperdoll/pdarc.htm
The United States Historical Society offers a new historically based paper doll each month from artist Lucinda Cunningham Durbin. Dolls are in full color and include clothes.

MARILEE'S PAPER DOLL PAGE
http://www.ameritech.net/users/macler/paperdolls.html
Marilee offers many dolls that you can print, plus a huge list of links to other paper doll sites on the Web. She also offers information on software for making paper dolls. This is a wonderful site with origami paper dolls, adult dolls, teenaged ones, and even animal paper dolls.

To Print Online Paper Dolls, wait until the Web page loads completely. In Netscape the "snow" in the corner of the Netscape logo will stop falling. In Internet Explorer the "world" logo will stop spinning when the page is loaded. Then use your browser's File/Print command to print the page. Print the page on heavy stock paper. Use tiny scissors, such as needle-nosed embroidery scissors, to cut the doll. You can glue the doll to cardboard with a can of spray glue. Press it between heavy books to flatten it. You can also laminate the doll by taking it to a copy store.

PAPER DOLL COLLECTING AT ABOUT.COM
http://collectdolls.about.com/msub13.htm
Doll maven Katie Kangas at About.com offers a wonderful collection of features and links to paper-doll collecting sites around the Net, including Patty Duke and Judy Garland paper dolls, fashion-magazine paper dolls, and more.

BARBIE PAPER DOLLS

http://www.barbie.com/collectors/justforfun/fashionshow/paper_dolls/index.html

*The home of Barbie (**http://www.barbie.com**) offers Barbie, plus her outfits and accessories.*

THE SHIRLEY TEMPLE COLLECTION

http://www.foxhome.com/shirley/html/doll/dollf.html

Print out Shirley and her outfits for Heidi, Rebecca, and the Princess at this site from Twentieth Century Home Fox Entertainment. The site includes directions for gluing and folding.

PAPER DOLL UNIVERSITY

http://paperdoll.hypermart.net

You'll find many printable paper dolls to color and decorate here.

DESIGN YOUR OWN FASHIONS WITH PRINT AND COLOR PAPER DOLLS

http://www.funorama.com/dolls.html

QUARTERBACK CUT-OUT AND ACTION FIGURES

http://www.funorama.com/qbclub.html

*Funorama offers dolls and clothes for you to print. You need Adobe Acrobat (**http://www.adobe.com**).*

Created and actively maintained by Dov Sherman

Paper Dolls for Your Computer from the World of Japanese Anime

You're probably familiar with the wild style of Japanese anime cartoon art. The Big Kiss Page: Paper Dolls for Your Computer (**http://otakuworld.com/kiss/**) run by Dov Sherman at Otaku World (**http://otakuworld.com**) offers hundreds of anime-style dolls that you can download with clothes and accessories that you can change. Once you download them you can play with them offline. The name "Kiss" hails from a Japanese term for playing dress-up. You can view hundreds of cartoon dolls online and select clothing for them. In order to view and dress the dolls you need to download the Kiss viewer. There's information on how to do this at the site, but this is definitely something for parents to configure. Kiss viewers are available for many different kinds of computers, including Macintosh and Amiga, but some are glitchy. Once you install the viewer you can preview and download cartoon dolls from the site. While most of the dolls are kids-oriented, some are adult-oriented, and adults will want to preview these electronic paper dolls before letting the kids sit down at the computer. (Click on all the "hanger" icons in the Kiss viewer to check what's hiding in the closets.) You can select the All Ages feature to screen dolls, but you'll still want to check them out yourself before giving them to the kids. Don't be deterred; some of the dolls and their clothes really are cute.

CHAPTER 8

Free How-Tos
for Making Paper
Airplanes
and Kites

If you've ever sat in the back of a classroom and pondered whether giving that paper airplane a bit of a tail fin would allow it to fly closer to the blackboard, or gazed out the window on a gusty day and tried to imagine yourself as a kite playing among the clouds, these Web sites are for you. They'll help you fold your math paper into a work of aeronautical perfection, and ensure that your kites are works of art as well as bold experiments in flight.

 Free Paper Airplane Folding Help

THE PAPER AIRPLANE HANGAR
http://www.tycs.demon.co.uk/planes
Ben Yeomans offers paper airplane safety tips, hints on making and flying paper planes, and a guide to building them correctly.

PAPER AIRPLANES
http://members.globalpac.com/frog/Parplane.html
Jared, a 17-year-old ham radio operator, provides instructions for folding three "cool" paper airplanes and one "very cool" paper helicopter.

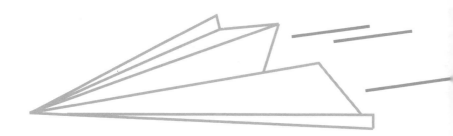

 WORLD RECORD PAPER AIRPLANE

http://www.workmanweb.com/plane.html

*Download the folding instructions for Ken Blackburn's 1994
Guiness world record-setting paper airplane, and copies of the
plane, courtesy of Blackburn's publisher Workman Publishing.*

JACOB'S PAPER PLANE PAGE

http://www.inlink.com/~jennings/paperpla.html

*Nine-year-old Jacob shares directions for two of his favorite
airplanes.*

TO FLY IS EVERYTHING

http://hawaii.cogsci.uiuc.edu/invent/air_main.shtml

*Visit this virtual museum at the University of Hawaii, which
introduces you to the invention of flight, and tells you how
planes fly.*

SABERTOOTH: A PAPER AIRPLANE

http://pantheon.cis.yale.edu/~cphung/saber.html

*Chou Hung, scientist at Yale, offers directions for folding his
favorite airplane.*

THE PHOENIX SKY HARBOR INTERNATIONAL AIRPORT: KIDS SECTION

http://www.phxskyharbor.com/skyharbr/kids/index.html

*Learn how to fold a "Roller," a "Whirly-Bird," an "Aero-Glider,"
and a "Speed Glider." And learn how real planes get off the
ground in Arizona.*

BUILD THE BEST PAPER AIRPLANE IN THE WORLD

http://www.zurqui.co.cr/crinfocus/paper/airplane.html

Michael O'Reilly gives instructions for folding the DC-3 of paper airplanes.

© 1999 Michael O'Reilly

 ## GINMEE TECH: FREE PAPER AIRPLANES

http://www.webcom.com/gmt/freeplane.html

Print and create Star Fighter and X-Fighter airplanes.

BUILDING THE EGRET

http://www.friend.ly.net/scoop/activity/airplact.html

(There is a period between "friend" and "ly" in the above URL, strange as it may seem.) These instructions come from Norman Schmidt's "Best Ever Paper Airplanes" by Sterling Publishing Co.

LEARN2 MAKE PAPER AIRPLANES

http://209.24.233.206/06/0646/0646.html

Learn2.Com offers help for the paper-airplane challenged.

Download Software to Make Super Paper Airplanes. You can download free trial versions of special software for making paper airplanes from KittyHawk Software. With Paper Air Force (**http://www.khs.com/khs/paf/paperair.htm**) you can create realistic planes. The Greatest Paper Airplanes (**http://www.khs.com/khs/aboutgpa.htm**) shows you how to fold paper airplanes with realistic 3D illustrations. Both are available for Windows and Mac.

Free Kite-Making How-Tos

20 KIDS, 20 KITES, 20 MINUTES
http://www.aloha.net/%7Ebigwind/20kidskites.html

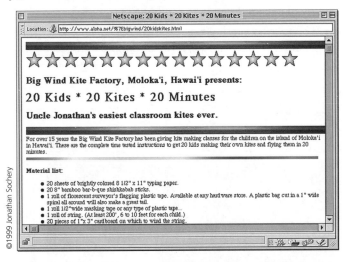

Visit The Big Wind Kite Factory on the island of Molokai in Hawaii to learn how to take 20 kids and get them to make 20 kites in 20 minutes.

EXETER KITE CENTRAL
http://www.ex.ac.uk/~jastaple/kites.html
John Staplehurst offers directions for making a paper sled kite.

THE BROXXES BASIC BOX KITE
http://sound.net/~kiteguy/kidspage/boxkite.htm
Retired Kansas teacher Dave Ellis offers instruction and encouragement on kite making. His site offers directions from the American Kitefliers Association.

LEARN TO MAKE A KITE
http://www.learn2.com/04/0479/04791.html
Learn the basics of kite making from Learn2.Com.

BUILD YOUR OWN TETRAHEDRON KITE
http://www.ttl.dsu.edu/woodburg/building.htm
Glenda Woodburn's sixth grade class at Buchanan Elementary School in Pierre, South Dakota provides thorough instructions on building a tetrahedron kite.

Web page created by Glenda Woodburn 1997

(HOW-TO) GO AND FLY A KITE!

http://www.interlog.com/~excells/kites

Jen Chan offers instructions for building a diamond kite, along with a history of kites, a discussion of how kites fly, and other information.

HOW TO MAKE A HEADSTICK KITE

http://cyberfair.gsn.org/gprep/make.kites.html

The primary seven students at St. George's Preparatory School in Bermuda offer instructions on how to make this aeronautical wonder.

CHARLIE CHARLTON'S KITE SITE

http://www.personal.u-net.com/~akg

Charlie and his son in Liverpool, England share plans for making a number of marvelous kites, including insights on painting them. Truly a site for kite fanatics!

© 1999 Charlie Charlton

KITE FLYER'S SITE

http://www.kfs.org/kites

Andrew Beattie offers over 500 links to kite information around the Web.

CLEM'S HOMEMADE NEWSPAPER KITE PAGE

http://www.clem.freeserve.co.uk

Web page created by David Clements. Drawings by Ian Clements.

"Clem" in the United Kingdom provides instructions for making a kite with newspaper or a brown bag and scissors.

THE KITE GUY

http://www.sound.net/~kiteguy

KIDKITEWEB

http://www.sound.net/~buckchil/KKWeb

Buck Childers in Canada offers a wonderful selection of kite information and links.

free Origami How-Tos

Maybe you have a friend like this: his mother gives him a shopping list and he comes home with it folded into a bird. At dinner his paper napkin twists itself into a creased boat. His school papers often emerge from his pocket as flowers. Origami, the Japanese art of paper folding, is the magic of transforming the commonplace slip of paper into a new little world. Many mathematicians are origami fans, for origami shares its principles with the mathematics of folding and transforming space. Through these Web sites you'll learn more about this quirky, delicate art. And soon flowers maybe unfolding from your pocket.

THE GARDEN OF ORIGAMI
http://ccwf.cc.utexas.edu/~vbeatty/origami/gate2.html
This is one of the most beautiful origami sites on the Web. Victoria Beatty at the University of Texas offers how-tos, insights, and many lovely pictures.

ORIGAMI USA
http://www.origami-usa.org
You'll find instructions, puzzles, and membership information in the Web site of this club for origami fans. The site also offers an origami mailing list and an archive of information relating to origami.

ANDY'S ORIGAMI PAGE
http://carpo.home.mindspring.com/AndysOrigamiPage/diagrams.htm
Andy Carpenter offers diagrams for folding sheep, squirrels, and birds. You need Adobe Acrobat to read them.

JASPER'S GUIDE TO PAPER FOLDING TECHNIQUES

http://home.earthlink.net/~jpaulsen/origami/tutorial

You'll find directions on making dozens of origami shapes including a swan, pirate, pinwheel, crane, and more in this collection of origami step-by-steps collected from origami fans around the Internet. The site is maintained by John Paulsen.

SY'S PAPER FOLDING PAGE

http://www.erols.com/sychen1/pprfld.html

Shi-Yew Chen shares his paper-folded creations and offers downloadable instructions for folding boats, a pyramid, and a pumpkin face.

JOSEPH WU'S ORIGAMI PAGE

http://www.origami.vancouver.bc.ca

Wu shares lots of knowledge and advice on origami, and offers photos of his work.

FABRIC ORIGAMI WORKSHOP

http://www.owt.com/gdscott

Glenda Scott describes how to make origami out of fabric.

RING OF ORIGAMI SITES

http://www.angelfire.com/la/Lal

Amy Huang is ringmaster to this collection of origami sites. Scroll down to the bottom of the page to visit more origami Web sites.

ORIGAMI MATHEMATICS

http://chasm.merrimack.edu/~thull/OrigamiMath.html

Tom Hull discusses the mathematics of paper folding on his site, and explains how to fold the five intersecting tetradedra.

BARF: THE BAY AREA RAPID FOLDERS
http://www.krmusic.com/barfup/barf.htm
*This San Francisco group of origami enthusiasts offers nifty
diagrams for folding a violin, a surfer on a wave and, of all
things, a chocolate-covered ant.*

 ## FASCINATING FOLDS
http://www.fascinating-folds.com/welcome.htm
*They bill themselves as the "world's largest supplier of origami
and paper arts products."*

JANE HAMILTON'S LIST OF ORIGAMI SOURCES
http://www.concentric.net/~mikeinnj/orisrc.shtml
*Jane has compiled a huge, huge list of origami resources and
supplies, both on the Web and off.*

WHY CHILDREN AROUND THE WORLD FOLD CRANES FOR PEACE

When 12-year-old Sadako Sasaki lay ill in the hospital one of her classmates brought her an origami crane. She told Sadako that cranes can grant wishes, and a person who folds a

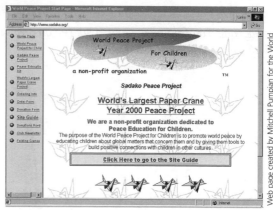

Web page created by Mitchell Pumpian for the World Peace Project for Children

thousand of them will have her wish granted if she wishes it with each crane she folds. So Sadako began folding cranes, wishing to get well. But the young survivor of the Hiroshima atomic blast died. When her classmates learned that she had folded 644 cranes they folded the rest for her, wishing for peace. Many of her friends went on to form the Paper Crane Club to raise money for a Children's Peace Monument in Hiroshima. Today children around the world fold cranes—to send to the monument, and to send to world leaders to remind them that children wish for peace. There are many, many Web sites where you can read about these efforts, as well as learn how to fold cranes. Here are just a few:

- WORLD PEACE PROJECT
  http://www.sadako.org

- VICTORIA BEATTY'S GARDEN OF ORIGAMI
  http://ccwf.cc.utexas.edu/~vbeatty/origami/learning/peace.html

- THOUSAND CRANES PEACE NETWORK
  http://rosella.apana.org.au/~mlb/cranes/index.htm

- CRANES FOR PEACE
  http://www.he.net/~sparker/cranes.html

free Drawing
and Art History
Lessons
for Budding Artists

Thinking of mailing a drawing to one of those art schools that advertise on TV? Save the stamp and surf the Web for free drawing lessons. You'll find illustrated instructions on how to sketch with pastels, how to render with charcoal, and how to paint like an Impressionist. There are even Web sites that offer cartooning tutorials. And if you're confused about what "art" is to begin with (don't worry, we all are), you'll find Web sites that can fill you in on history and appreciation of art.

Free Drawing and Painting Lessons for Kids (and Their Teachers)

ART EDUCATION: FREE OIL PAINTING LESSON
http://www.1art.com/tips.htm
Alexei L. Antonov explains how to paint an apple, Flemish style.

ART STUDIO CHALKBOARD
http://www.saumag.edu/art/studio/chalkboard.html
Ralph Larmann from the Southern Arkansas University Art Department teaches drawing and painting fundamentals.

DRAW AND COLOR WITH UNCLE FRED
http://www.unclefred.com/index.html
Follow step-by-step instructions for drawing a rabbit, penguin, and a surfer.

🛒 DRAW DINO BABY BY MARK KISTLER

http://www.drawwithmark.com/3dlessns/dinobaby/dinobab2.htm

MARK KISTLER'S ELECTRONIC PENCIL POWER PLAYGROUND

http://www.drawwithmark.com

MARK KISTLER'S IMAGINATION STATION

http://www.draw3d.com

Mark is a Web drawing teacher extraordinare. He'll teach you how to draw a baby dinosaur, and teach you the 12 secrets of drawing in three dimensions, including shading, overlapping, and foreshortening. You select a drawing, then learn how to draw it. Dennis Dawn created this wonderful site.

CRAYOLA'S ART EDUCATION

http://www.crayola.com:80/art_education/techniques/home.html

The makers of crayons offer tips on coloring with crayons, markers, paint, and pencils.

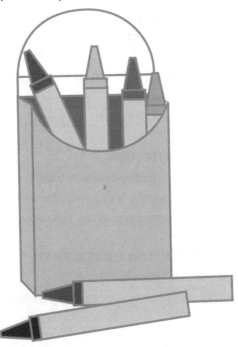

FREE ART AND DRAWING LESSONS FROM HOME SCHOOL ARTS

http://www.homeschoolarts.com/main.htm

The lessons on watercolor, perspective color pencil, pen and ink, and pastels are free, but you need to sign up and obtain a password—be sure to ask mom or dad before you do.

THE INCREDIBLE ART DEPARTMENT

http://www.artswire.org/kenroar/lessons/lessons.html

Founded by Ken Rohrer and updated by Paul Bradley, the art Web site offers a wide range of "lessons" for toddler artists through high school ones.

KALEIDOSCOPE PAINTER

http://www.ben2.ucla.edu/~permadi/java/spaint/spaint.html

Remember playing with a Spirograph as a kid? F. Permadi created this nifty program which is similar. Drag your mouse around the screen to create kaleidoscopic designs.

KINDERART: ARTS AND CRAFTS FOR KIDS OF ALL AGES

http://www.kinderart.com/drawing

Andrea Mulder-Slater and Jantje Mulder offer lessons in crayon etching, crayon resist, chalk and glue drawing, ink drawing, and wet chalk painting. They even show you how to create monsters through the use of textures. Teachers will also find a lot of ideas at this site.

PAINTING PROJECTS

http://www.paintingmag.com/projects/index.htm

Painting Magazine Online (**http://www.paintingmag.com**) *offers new projects each month. Some previous projects: a faux finish clock, pansy curtains, and four ways to create texture with watercolor paints.*

WATERCOLOR FLORAL DEMO

http://www3.edgenet.net/artistwc/demo.htm

George Simmons takes you through the steps of painting gladiolus in watercolor.

WATERCOLOR WEB

http://members.aol.com/WCstudio/index.html

You'll find articles, hints, and tips for the watercolorist.

🛒 WINDSOW AND NEWTON—LEARN TO PAINT

http://www.winsornewton.com

You'll find water, acrylic, and oil painting lessons and a tips and techniques section. You'll also find how-tos on subjects like how to tint black-and-white photographs with watercolors (like they used to do before color cameras).

Visit the National Park Service for Art!

The Web site of The National Park Service offers a beautiful virtual exhibit of the work of Thomas Moran, whose watercolors of Yellowstone inspired Congress to protect it as a national park (**http://www.cr.nps.gov/csd/exhibits/moran**). While you're there head to its Pieces of the Past features (**http://www.cr.nps.gov/pastfeat.htm**) for other exhibits, like the one on Frederick Douglas. Teachers will appreciate Tools for Teachers (**http://www.cr.nps.gov/toolsfor.htm**) which offers more information and links on American history.

Free Art Lessons for the Budding Cartoonist

EMMETT SCOTT'S CARTOON CORNER
http://www.cartooncorner.com
Emmett explains how to draw cartoons, and also offers puzzles and other features.

COMICS CRAZY.COM
http://www.comicscrazy.com
You'll find drawing tutorials, plus cartoon superheroes at this huge Web site from Robert Shelley, Jr.

CARTOONING LESSONS FROM GLEN WYAND
http://www.sara-jordan.com/cartoon/lesson1.html
Sara Jordan's Edu-Mart offers cartooning lessons from artist Glen Wyand.

HOT DRAWING TIPS FROM RADICALMAN
http://www.radicalman.com/tips/main.htm
RadicalMan offers over 130 cartoon drawing tips on topics like how to draw a horizon line, how to create depth and the illusion of movement, and how to make far-off objects look realistic.

Art History and Appreciation Lessons for All Ages

THE ALPHABET OF ART

http://www.atl.mindspring.com/~massa/alphabet.html

Learn principles of design, such as line, texture, and value, at this Web site from Guidance Communications, Inc.

A. PINTURA: ART DETECTIVE

http://www.eduweb.com/pintura

Learn about art history while playing detective at this fun site from Educational Web Adventures. It also includes teachers' resources.

ART, DESIGN, AND VISUAL THINKING

http://char.txa.cornell.edu/zbs/webdocs

We love this site from Cornell University! Learn about the language of design, the media of design—such as painting, drawing, printmaking, textiles—the evolution of fine arts, dress, decorative arts, and more. This amazing site includes extensive study guides.

ARTLEX—THE DICTIONARY OF VISUAL ART

http://www.artlex.com

You'll find definitions of almost 3,000 art terms for artists, students, and teachers.

ART NOW GALLERY GUIDE ONLINE

http://www.gallery-guide.com/content/current

This wonderful Web site from Art Now, Inc. includes links to over 1,500 art galleries, museums, and other art resources on the Web.

EXPLORE ART

http://members.aol.com/powers8696/artindex.html

Connie M. Powers gives art classes on her Web site with lessons for children, art teachers, and parents on Picasso, Cézanne, Grandma Moses, and other artists. You'll find discussions of their work, a gallery, and links to other Web resources on each artist.

EYES ON ART

http://www.kn.pacbell.com/wired/art2

Tom March created this interactive site to help visitors explore the concept of art and decide what is good art.

THE GETTY MUSEUM'S ARTS EDNET

http://www.artsednet.getty.edu

You'll find a fantastic selection of art lesson plans for elementary, middle, and high school students from the Getty.

INSIDE ART: AN ART HISTORY GAME

http://www.eduweb.com/insideart/index.html

Play an art history game to learn about what art is all about, courtesy of Educational Web Adventures and Teachers' Resources.

THE ONLINE VISUAL LITERACY PROJECT

http://www.pomona.edu/visual-lit/intro/intro.html

Learn about the fundamentals of visual communication, including the language of dots, color, and shape, from Pomona College, Claremont, California.

THE REFRIGERATOR: THE CHILDREN'S ONLINE GALLERY

http://web.aimnet.com/~jennings/refrigerator/index.html

Mike Jennings runs this site where visitors can appreciate other children's art.

SANFORD'S ART ADVENTURES

http://www.sanford-artedventures.com

Join Carmine Chameleon in "Color Theory vs. Dr. Gray and His Dechromatizer," a very nifty interactive art adventure from Educational Web Adventures.

VIRTUAL MUSEUM FIELD TRIP

http://members.aol.com/TINATOMATO/VirtualMuseumFieldTrip.html

Tina Marie of San Antonio, Texas created this "virtual field trip" of art museums around the world.

THE WORLD OF ESCHER

http://www.WorldOfEscher.com

You can view a gallery of lithographs by master illusionist
M.C. Escher, as well as read articles about his art and his life at
this amazing site.

Head to the Exploratorium for Unique Web Art Experiences

The Museum of Art, Science, and Human Perception (**http://www.exploratorium.org**), located in San Francisco, features over 650 interactive hands-on exhibits that teach visitors about art as well as science. You'll find similar fun on the museum's Web site. Build a scale model of the solar system, learn about memory, explore the creation of chocolate, and tap into some of the most amazing and illuminating sites on the Web.

You Can't Paint Without Music! Head to the Eyeneer Music Archives

(**http://www.eyeneer.com**) for links to contemporary classic, new jazz, and American music around the Web. In the site's International Music Archive you'll find photos, sound samples, and descriptions of music and instruments.

free Rubber Stamping and Scrapbooking Fun

R ubber stamps are great! An ink pad and a flick of the wrist are all you need to stamp miniature works of art on notecards, letters, school papers, even lunch bags. Scribble a message under the stamping, or embellish it with your own cartooning and you've left a personal statement that can bring a smile or chuckle. Best of all, no artistic talent is necessary. The Web is a great place to indulge your rubber stamping passion. You'll find Web sites that sell rubber stamps and pads, plus many that offer ideas and tutorials on rubber-stamping your way to happiness. If scrapbooking is your pleasure, you'll find Web sites full of advice, inspiration—and even adventure.

 Free Rubber Stamping How-Tos and Talk

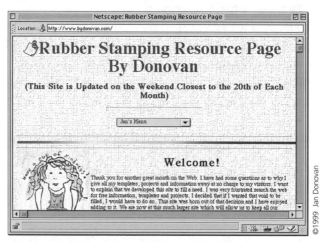

©1999 Jan Donovan

RUBBER STAMPING RESOURCE PAGE

http://www.bydonovan.com

Jan Donovan offers directions for all kinds of nifty projects, like a Venetian blinds card, plus stamping tips and more.

STAMPIN' AND SCRAPPIN'

http://www.stampinscrappin.com

Talk stamping with other fanatics. You'll find message boards, plus tips and more to do.

"HOW TO MAKE A RUBBER STAMP" BY DER MAD STAMPER

http://members.aol.com/Letterboxr/carving.html

You'll find illustrated directions for carving erasers to make rubber stamps.

INK SPOT RUBBER STAMPING PAGE

http://www.aone.com/~edc97/stamper

Sign up for a free catalog and the stamp of the month newsletter.

RUBBER STAMPEDE

http://www.rstampede.com

You'll find lots of basic stamping advice, plus tips and how-tos.

DRAGONHOME'S RUBBER STAMPING PAGE

http://www.littlebit.com/rubber1.htm

Judith Perry offers tips, how-tos, and an extensive list of links to other stamping Web sites. You'll even find a rubber-stamping screen saver to download.

🛒 THE STAMPING PLACE: TIPS AND TECHNIQUES

http://www.stampin.com/tips.htm

You'll find all kinds of how-tos on subjects such as heat embossing, markers, 3D techniques, stained-glass techniques, background techniques, and much more.

RUBBER STAMPING PAGE

http://www.xmission.com/~jmabunga/stamp.htm

John D. Mabunga offers a glossary, tips, FAQs, chat channel, and lots more fun for stampers.

🛒 THE ART OF EMBOSSING

http://www.atlanticstampers.com/how1.htm

Step-by-step instructions from the Atlantic Stampers.

🛒 CREATIVE STAMPING—THE BASICS

http://www.sgmweb.net/creastamp/basics.htm

Betty and Steve explain the basics of rubber stamping.

SCRAPBOOK, RUBBER STAMPING, AND PAPER ARTS
http://www.22cool.com
Ooh! This is one cool site! You'll find loads of articles, plus chat and a whole lot more from the Two Too Cool Mail Guys.

THE RUBBER STAMPING HOME PAGE FROM DELPHI
http://www0.delphi.com/RUBBER
There are all sorts of stamping fun going on in this big Web site from Delphi. You'll find swaps, projects, how-tos, and much more.

THE RUBBER STAMPER: A MAGAZINE FOR RUBBER STAMP ENTHUSIASTS
http://www.rubberstamper.com
You'll find free how-tos at the site of this magazine.

STAMP OASIS
http://www.stampoasis.com/home3.html
Take a virtual stroll of this Las Vegas store—and look for the freebies.

Free Scrapbooking How-Tos

SCRAP HAPPY SCRAPBOOKS
http://www.telepath.com/bcarson/scrap_happy/indexo.html
You'll find lots of information here on creating scrapbooks—plus freebies like fonts, instruction sheets, and seasonal ideas. The site also offers a great collection of links into the "Internet scrapbooking community."

THE SCRAPBOOK IDEA NETWORK
http://www.learn2scrapbook.com/index.html
This is the ultimate Web site for scrapbook makers. Learn about the history of scrapbook making, visit forums, find out about the latest products, and learn new techniques. Anamarie Seidel details instructions to get you started, and she includes monthly updates.

THE SCRAPBOOK ADDICT HOME PAGE

http://members.tripod.com/~tln123/luv2scrap.html

Once you start you can't stop. That's the idea behind the Scrapbook Addict. You'll find layout ideas, a mailing list, and lots of links to the Web sites of other scrapbookers, plus ideas on how to make scrapbooks of your children's memorabilia.

DO IT YOURSELF SCRAPBOOKING

http://members.aol.com/scrappinpc/index.html

ScrappinPC, a.k.a. Jess, offers tips, how-tos, and clipart to adorn your scrapbook.

JANGLE.COM

http://www.jangle.com

Leap into the world of scrapbooking on the Web at this super site where you'll find layout ideas, tips, articles, and conversations about scrapbooking. Click "Rubber Inklings" for articles and tips for rubber stamping.

REMEMBER ME SCRAPBOOKING

http://www.remembermesb.com/layouts/laykid.htm

You'll find free layouts for kids' scrapbooks, plus chatting, and many ideas.

AMERICAN TRADITIONAL STENCILS

http://www.amtrad-stencil.com

Visit the Projects Page for tutorials on memory album stamping.

Join the Scrapbook WebRing! Visit other scrap-booking Web pages by surfing the SCRAPBOOK WEBRING (**http://home1.gte.net/saraka4/webring.htm**) run by Dynail Miller. You don't need to "join" the ring to explore the sites. Merely select the List of Sites and start surfing.

More Scrapbooking Tips at About.com You'll find some terrific articles on scrapbooking young children's memories at About.com's Baby & Toddler Parenting center (**http://babyparenting.about.com**). Head to the "library" for past articles.

Why Not Try to Bind Your Scrapbooks?

Why buy scrapbooks made by someone else when you can make your own books? Learn the art of bookbinding (it's not hard) at these wonderful Web sites:

DOUGLAS W. JONES ON BOOKBINDING
http://www.cs.uiowa.edu/~jones/book

SHEILA SUMMERS' BASIC BOOKBINDING TUTORIAL
http://holly.colostate.edu/~sheilas

free Tole Painting and Decoupage Tutorials

Nothing transforms a ho-hum piece of furniture like a bit of paint or decoupage. Go to a garage sale; pick up a dorky-looking hand-hewn dresser or chair from the '60s. Don't spend more than a dollar or two. Paint it and apply some of the tutorials you'll find on these Web sites. You'll be amazed at how you can transform your bedroom with something so simple. That's what we did when we were teens. And our parents still won't let us forget it. "I can't believe I let you paint the head of your bed that bright yellow and paint all those weird flowers all over it when you were sixteen!" they still carp. Ah, but we had such fun doing it! In fact, we still do that sort of thing as adults (much to our husbands' despair).

Free Decorative Painting How-Tos

http://www.art2art.net/a2a/projectsheets.html
Directions for stenciling, tole and other decorative painting projects are yours on this wonderful site. The projects call for Art2Art products, but you can use other painting products if you prefer.

🛒 DECOR DELIGHTS: TOLE AND DECORATIVE PAINTING

http://www.decordelights.com

You'll find beautiful patterns and tole lessons on this comprehensive site. You'll learn about wood preparation, varnishing, brush strokes, and stippling.

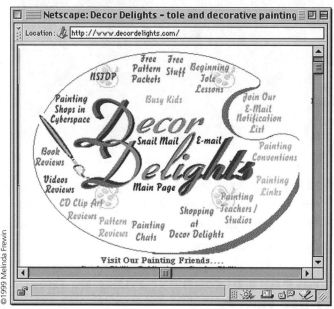

🛒 DOWNLOADABLE TOLE PAINTING PROJECTS FROM STONE BRIDGE COLLECTION

http://www.stonebridgecoll.com/packets.html

You'll find dozens of gorgeous designs for painting plates, chests, boxes, and more. You can download the full-sized drawings, plus directions and lists of needed paints and brushes.

JO SONJA'S ARTIST'S COMPANION BOOKLET

http://www.stonebridgecoll.com/josonja/js_book.html

Also from the Stone Bridge Collection, this online guide provides excellent instruction for using Jo Sonja's Artist Colors.

BUSY BRUSHES DOT COM
http://www.busybrushes.com

This is a cool site! You'll find a classroom with how-tos on painting roses, lilacs, leaves, and more. Learn how to apply fabric to wood. There's also a lovely selection of free patterns, a mailing list, bulletin board, and more.

🛒 TOLE AND DECORATIVE PAINTING FROM BUSY BEE CRAFTS
http://www.busybee.ns.ca

Gloria Charest shares free patterns such as a little girl ring holder and a Santa lightbulb ornament.

TOLENET
http://www.tolenet.com

One of the most beautiful painting sites on the Net, ToleNet offers painterly chats, book and product reviews, lessons, and lots of beautiful free patterns.

TOLE AND DECORATIVE PAINTING ON THE WEB
http://members.home.net/barkhous/index.html

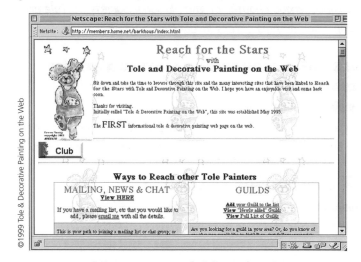

Jeannine from Ontario, Canada shares many beautiful projects. She also answers frequently asked questions and provides links to newsgroups, guilds, chats, guilds, and suppliers.

TOLE PAINTING MESSAGE BOARD
http://www.craftmall.com/forums/tolepaint/index.html
Post your tole-related questions here at this site sponsored by the Craft Mall.

TOLE AND DECORATIVE PAINTING IDEAS BY ERIKA FREI
http://www.hurricane.net/~pattern
This commercial site includes a cute, free pattern for Reindeer Rudy.

TOLE WORLD
http://www.stonebridgecoll.com/toleworl/mag1/toleworl.htm
You'll find information about the bimonthly magazine published by EGW Publishing Co., plus features and more.

ENCHANTED PAINTERS

http://www.thuntek.net/~rhardy/paint

The Albuquerque chapter of the National Society of Tole and Decorative Painters offers lovely free patterns.

TOLE AND DECORATIVE PAINTING ARTIST'S RESOURCE

http://www.tolenet.com/index.html

This site, sponsored by Ken Tera, hosts a mailing list for decorative painters with over a thousand members.

🛒 LUCI RITCHIE CRAFTPALS

http://craftpals.org/lritchie/index.html

You'll find tips and free patterns from Luci Ritchie.

NATIONAL SOCIETY OF TOLE AND DECORATIVE PAINTING

http://www.decorativepainters.com/publication.htm

You'll find information about membership, a link to the Tru Color Systems software, and other features.

DECORATIVE PAINTING: THE CREATIVE ARTIST

http://creativeartist.com

Judy Miller offers a lovely selection of free painting patterns, a bulletin board, chat room, mailing list, postcards, and more.

Web site created and designed by Fall River Decorative Arts

 DELTA CRAFTS

http://www.deltacrafts.com/index_normal.asp

Click the Free Stuff, Project Ideas, or Just for Kids icons for loads of free painting project how-tos, from "Funky Rose Mugs" to "Autographed Pillowcases."

 **Use Software to Keep Track of Your Paint Stuff** You can keep track of your magazines, books, packets, sales, and more with Decorative Painter Database (**http://www.simp-list.com**) from Simp-List Software. You can download a demo from its Web site. It's available in both PC and Mac flavors.

 Free Decoupage How-Tos

MAKESTUFF: MAKE VICTORIAN BOXES

http://www.makestuff.com/decoupage_boxes.html

DECOUPAGE GIFTS

http://www.makingfriends.com/decopage.htm

DECOUPAGE MAGNETS

from Beverly's Craft & Fabric Store
http://www.beverlys.com/phomag.htm

CRAFT CREATIONS, LTD.

http://www.craftcreations.com/Articles/articles.html

Many free craft projects, including instructions for several beautiful 3D decoupage projects.

CHAPTER 13

free
Polymer Clay,
Beading, and
Jewelry-Making
How-Tos

I t may be called clay, but Polymer clay isn't from the earth. It was actually invented in Germany around 1930 and is made of PVC, or polyvinyl chloride—the same stuff found in modern plumbing—suspended in a plasticizer. You can find it in crafts stores under the name FIMO. It comes in hundreds of colors and is great for making beads, jewelry, ornaments, and other crafty things, like dolls' heads. It's so much better than the salt dough we loved to sculpt as teens. And unlike real clay you don't need to bake it at volcanic temperatures. In fact, you can even fire it in a toaster oven. It's certified as non-toxic. Even so, keep it far from youngsters who might put it in their mouth.

 Free Polymer Clay How-Tos

POLYMER CLAY CENTRAL ON DELPHI
http://www.delphi.com/polymerclay/pcc/opening.html
Leigh Ross hosts this wonderful Web site at Delphi, where you'll find project how-tos, tips, ideas, and more.

"POLYMER CLAY: A LACE CANE" BY LEIGH ROSS
http://www0.delphi.com/crafts/lacecane.html
Leigh explains a technique for rolling polymer into a multi-colored "cane" that you can cut into beads and other shapes.

THE POLYMER CLAY SPOT

http://www.jaedworks.com/clayspot

Jeanne A. E. DeVoto shares her techniques, explains how to imitate the look of stone, and answers your questions. Click the "Newbie Zone" to get help if you've just started sculpting.

SCULPEY FAMILY OF POLYMER CLAY PRODUCTS

http://www.sculpey.com/index.htm

You'll find instructions to projects such as a Santa lightbulb ornament and a heart-shaped picture frame. You'll also find tips and answers to common polymer questions.

POLYMER CLAY PROJECTS BY DONNA KATO

http://www.prairiecraft.com/projects.html

Prairie Craft Company offers polymer crafting advice and instructions for things such as fat pens and a mosaic egg on its project page.

PLANET FIMO PROJECT PAGE

http://www.fimozone.com/how.html

Barbara A. McGuire shares instructions for polymer clay projects at FimoZone (**http://www.fimozone.com**).

Join the Polymer Clay Web Ring! To surf Web sites devoted to polymer clay head to the Polymer Clay Ring (**http://www.cyberstreetfair. com/polyring. htm**). You don't need to "join" the ring to surf it. Scroll to the bottom of this page and select a random Web site to surf.

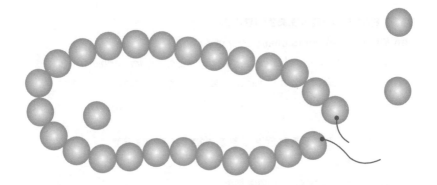

 Free How-Tos at Web Sites of Beading and Jewelry-Making Magazines

BEADING AND CLAY PROJECTS FROM JEWELRY CRAFTS MAGAZINE

http://jewelrycrafts.com/projects.html

JEWELRY CRAFTS MAGAZINE

http://jewelrycrafts.com

Jewelry Crafts offers pages of free instructions for beading and clay projects, for earrings, necklaces, bracelets, and pendants.

BEAD & BUTTON MAGAZINE

http://www2.beadandbutton.com/beadbutton/

You'll find lots of free tutorials, especially for jewelry making, from the magazine from Kalmbach Publishing.

THE BEADAHOLIC QUARTERLY

http://members.tripod.com/~auroram

Aurora Mathews publishes a free Web-based magazine with patterns, instructions, and beading articles.

ETCETERA

http://www.eebeads.com/Webzine

This bi-monthly beading e-zine from Carolyn S. Nehring offers a huge and growing selection of project how-tos.

More Free Beading and Jewelry-Making How-Tos

BEADWORK AT ABOUT.COM
http://beadwork.about.com/

You'll find an archive of beading how-tos, a chat room, a bulletin board, and lots of links to beading sites around the Web in this remarkable Site from About.com

JEWELRY-MAKING AT THE ABOUT.COM
http://jewelrymaking.about.com/index.htm

Tammy Powley runs this great site that includes lots of project how-tos on topics such as soldering, selecting tools, enameling, and casting. The site also offers help for modeling polymer clay and knotting macramé jewelry.

AUNT MOLLY'S BEAD STREET: FREE SEED BEADWORK PATTERNS AND PROJECTS
http://www.flash.net/~mjtafoya/home.htm

Mary J. Tafoya offers some very cool projects and a virtual classroom where you can learn about beading.

THE BEAD FAIRIES PAGE
http://www.mcs.net/~simone/beadfairies.html

Simone Oettinger runs this marvelous beading Web site. Make it your first stop for beading help on the Net.

FOCUSED ON BEADS: BEADING TECHNIQUES
http://www.halcyon.com/tarold/techniqs.htm

Learn looming, the daisy chain, and the peyote and square stitch at this neat site. It also offers free projects.

🛒 THE BEADIN' PATH

http://www.beadinpath.com/projects.htm

*You'll find tutorials for making
fashionable beaded
barrettes and ornaments.*

NATASHA BEADS

http://www.webhaven.com/crick/natasha1/index.htm

*Diana Crick offers illustrated instructions for making Natasha
Beads with mirror-image designs on all sides of the bead.*

CHAPTER 14

Free How-Tos for Puppet Making, Balloon Twisting, Juggling, and Magic

Do you want to make puppets? Do you want to twist balloons into the shape of parrots and dachshunds? Or maybe you'd like to master the crafts of magic or blowing colossal balloons. These Web sites will help you become the hit of your next party.

 Free Puppetry How-Tos

ANIMAL HAND PUPPETS
http://www.robinsfyi.com/crafts/handpuppets.htm
Robin offers how-tos for making a bear puppet, a cat puppet, a frog, and an owl.

THE PUPPETRY HOME PAGE
http://www.sagecraft.com/puppetry
Rose Sage offers one of the best sites on the Web for puppet-makers. You'll find information about puppetry organizations, festivals, and theaters, and of course how-tos. She also offers links to puppetry discussion groups.

HOW TO MAKE A PUPPET FOR AGES 3-5
http://www.era-publications.com.au/teacherpuppet.html
Josie McKinnon offers a finger-puppet pattern from her book Making Puppets.

MAKING A PUPPET PLAY

http://www.mitra.net.id/family/activity/pupplay.htm

Learn how to create a puppet play with instructions from creating a simple stage box and puppets to making backgrounds and writing your play script. From MitraNet.

CENTER FOR PUPPETRY ARTS

http://www.puppet.org/index.shtml

Chuck Robinson runs this Web site which includes many beautiful pictures of puppets from around the world.

NO STRINGS ATTACHED

http://www.foobar.co.uk/~drneil/Page1.html

Neil M. J. Burley explains how to make a simple puppet, how to perform in public, how to operate your puppet, and lots more.

🛒 STAGE HAND PUPPETS ACTIVITY PAGE

http://www3.ns.sympatico.ca/onstage/puppets/activity/index.html

You'll find free puppet patterns, such as an origami stick puppet, and lots of puppet performance tips—for instance, movement is a must!

REIMA'S PUPPET MINISTRY HOME PAGE
http://www.great.fi/~rei
Reima Honkasalo in Finland explains how to move a puppet, enter a stage, and more.

THE JIM HENSON COMPANY "VIRTUAL MUPPETEERING"
http://www.henson.com
The makers of the Muppets offer a "virtual muppeteering" page on which you can practice making the Muppets talk.

 Free Bubble-Making How-Tos

BUBBLE TOOLS
http://bubbles.org/html/tools.htm
*"Professor Bubbles" shows you how to make fabulous bubbles by using string, a hanger, other everyday household tools, and even your hands in this remarkable Web site devoted to bubble-making, Bubblesphere (**http://www.bubbles.org**).*

BIG BUBBLE MAGIC
http://www.wetrock.com/bbm.html
Kelly O'Neill gives the recipe and instructions for making big—we mean really big bubbles.

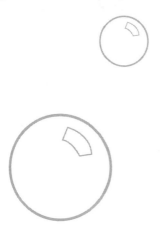

THE FRIENDS OF HAMILTON CHILDREN'S MUSEUM BIG BUBBLE

http://friends.ets.net/bubbles.htm

You'll find a recipe for bubble solution, plus instructions for the "super secret bubble stick."

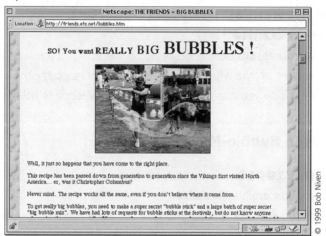

 Free Balloon Twisting How-Tos

BALLOON HQ, LLC

http://www.fooledya.com/balloon

You can practically hear the squeak, squeak of balloons being twisted into toy dogs as you tap into this great Web site from Balloon HQ, LLC. There are contests, FAQs, a mailing list and photos, and a downloadable guide that will have you twisting and pinching balloons into all types of creatures.

KIDS STUFF WITH MAGICAL BALLOON-DUDE DALE

http://www.mbd2.com/kidsstuff.htm

Balloon-dude Dale of Chicago offers step-by-step instructions for twisting balloons to create shapes including an airplane, dog, crocodile, and flying mouse.

Free Juggling Craft How-Tos

HOW TO JUGGLE
http://www.acm.uiuc.edu/webmonkeys/juggling/index.html
Chris Seguin explains how to juggle.

JUGGLING INFORMATION SERVICE
http://www.juggling.org
If you're a juggler or you want to learn how to become one, this site from Barry Bakalor is for you.

LEARN HOW TO JUGGLE
http://www.maths.tcd.ie/~nryan/juggle
Learn the basics of the "three ball cascade" and "how to show off" from Niall Ryan.

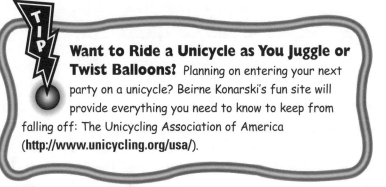

Want to Ride a Unicycle as You Juggle or Twist Balloons? Planning on entering your next party on a unicycle? Beirne Konarski's fun site will provide everything you need to know to keep from falling off: The Unicycling Association of America (**http://www.unicycling.org/usa/**).

 Free Magic Craft How-Tos

CONJOUR MAGIC
http://www.conjuror.com
Learn Houdini's rubber band secret, the vanishing knot, learn about the history of magic tricks—and how to craft the magic supplies you need at Neil Alexander's nifty Web spot. Remember that a good magician never reveals how the trick is done!

MAGIC INTERACTIVE

http://www.magic-interactive.com

You'll find plenty of tricks and illusions to baffle your friends, as well as a history of the sleight-of-hand trick and lots of conversations and games, in this site for amateur and professional magicians.

© 1999 Neil Alexander and Magic Happens Productions

THE MAGICIAN'S CORNER

http://www.ndirect.co.uk/~s.wilson/magic/index.html

The Magician's Corner, from S. Wilson in the United Kingdom, includes a special section on magic for kids. The "Ask the Mad Magician" feature gives you a chance to stump "Cookie" with your magic questions.

AN INTERNET MAGICLAND

http://fly.to/magicland

Dean Wilder's magic site offers help for beginning tricksters.

🛒 MAGIC TRICKS

http://www.magictricks.com

Learn sleight-of-hand tricks, read about the three unbreakable rules of magic, the 21 types of magic, and more at this wonderful site from Peter Monticup and MAGIC.

Get Answers to Your Mythology

Questions Need to know who Zeus was? Wondering who won the battle of Troy? Get answers to all your questions regarding mythology and folklore at Encyclopedia Mythia (**http://www.pantheon.org/ mythica**). This online encyclopedia covers Aztec, Chinese, Hindu, Native American, and many other types of mythology. Search it by name or use the comprehensive index.

CHAPTER 15

free Holiday Crafting How-Tos

What's more fun than getting together with a few friends over the holidays and making ornaments? Or helping your mom or dad weave a holiday wreath? The Web sites in this chapter offer many holiday crafting ideas for gifts you can make, decorations for your home or classroom, or for crafts you can simply enjoy making with family and friends over the holidays.

Free Big Holiday Crafting Web Sites

CRAFTS FOR KIDS AT ABOUT.COM
http://craftsforkids.about.com
About.Com offers crafting how-tos and links to holiday-themed craft projects around the Net, including ones for Mother's Day, Father's Day, St. Patrick's Day, and more.

CHRISTMAS AND HANUKKAH ACTIVITIES AT ABOUT.COM
http://birding.about.com/library/weekly/blxmas.htm
Christine Tarski, About.Com's birding guide, shares an assortment of articles and links for the holiday season. There's holiday clipart, gifts to make, and many games, crafts, and activities.

ANNIE'S LINKS TO HOLIDAY GRAPHICS

http://www.annieshomepage.com/holidaygraphics.html

Aunt Annie offers a big selection of graphic links organized by month.

KINDERART - SEASONAL THEMES

http://www.kinderart.com/seasons/dec.htm

Andrea Mulder-Slater and Jantje Mulder run this terrific site with Hanukkah, Christmas, and Kwanzaa projects.

HOLIDAYS ON THE NET

http://www.holidays.net

If you love to celebrate holidays, you'll want to bookmark this site. Studio Melizo lavishly celebrates Mardi Gras, the High Holy Days, Hanukkah, Ramadan, Easter, Christmas, and everything in between.

© 1999 Louie Volpe

HOLIDAY CRAFT IDEAS

http://www.netfix.com/poptart

Wendy Hogan has compiled a nifty assortment of craft projects and ideas.

ARTS AND CRAFTS

http://www.inmotion-pcs.com/amass/theboss/artsn.htm

You'll find plenty of Halloween, Thanksgiving, and Christmas projects to keep you busy at this site sponsored by In Motion.

CRAFTPALS CHILDREN'S HOLIDAY CRAFTS

http://craftpals.hypermart.net/kidcrafts.html

This lovely site is loaded with craft projects for many different holidays including Christmas, Easter, and Halloween. There are recipes, too.

INTERNATIONAL HOLIDAYS

http://www.rubicon.com/passport/holidays/holidays.htm

January 1 is New Years Day in the United States. But did you also know that it's Independence Day in Sudan? This interesting site by Kayleen Beard lists every holiday by month and offers insights into each.

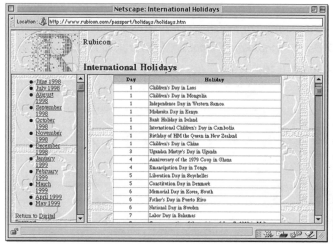

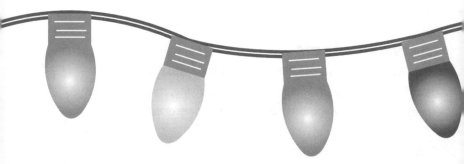

Travel Web Rings for More Holiday Fun

Many people put up Web sites for specific holidays. Often these sites are linked together in "rings." When you travel a Web ring you can visit linked sites in that ring at random. You don't need to join the ring in order to travel it. Click on its icon or the ring link at the bottom of member Web sites to hop from one Web site in the ring to another. You'll find some Web rings at the Web Ring home (**http://www.webring.org**). Here are the addresses of some holiday-themed Web rings:

SEASONS GREETINGS HOLIDAY WEBRING

http://www.webdesignbyjulie.com/jstevens/html/seasons_
greeting_webring.html

HAPPY HOLIDAYS WEBRING

http://members.tripod.com/~valerie815/holidays/webring.html

Need to Make a Bow but Don't Know How? Visit You Can Make Bows (**http://www.beakman.com/bow/bow.html**) where you'll see illustrated instructions from Jok Church for tying pretty ribbons on packages. Courtesy of Beakman's World (**http://www.beakman.com**).

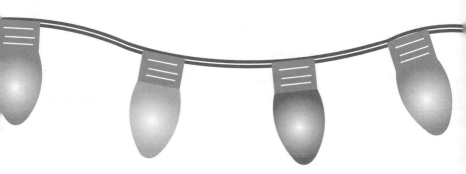

Free Christmas Crafting Web Sites

CHRISTMAS WITH READER'S DIGEST

http://www.rdchristmas.com/html/crafts/index.htm

You'll find directions for many holiday projects including gift tags, wrapping paper, an advent calendar, and a gingerbread cottage.

OFFRAY RIBBONS

http://www.offray.com/howto.html

Offray Ribbons offers directions on making bows, Christmas ornaments, and other beautiful holiday accessories.

CHRISTMAS CRAFTS AT KIDS DOMAIN

http://www.kidsdomain.com/holiday/xmas/craft.html

You'll find how-tos for lots of projects including a Santa's beard, felt ornaments, and paper-cone ornaments.

CHRISTMAS DECORATING

http://www.christmas98.com/dec_tips.html

The Internet Craft Fair offers 101 basket decorating ideas.

HOLIDAY GIFT WRAPPING IDEAS
http://www.christmas98.com/dec_wrap.html
Wrap your gift in brown craft paper, use binder twine as ribbon, tuck in a few pine, spruce, or holly sprigs. This is just one of the many ideas you'll find for gift-wrapping at the Internet Craft Fair.

NOT JUST FOR KIDS: CHRISTMAS, CHRISTMAS, CHRISTMAS
http://www.night.net/christmas
Cyberspace Christmas fun, including songs, games, links to other Web sites, and of course crafts.

CLAUS.COM
http://www.claus.com/village.html
What a wonderful and magical Web site! Visit Santa's toy factory, check your Naughty or Nice rating, e-mail Santa, and much more.

SANTA'S SECRET VILLAGE

http://www.northpole.com/main.html

Visit Santa's Reindeer Barn, Santa's den, the Clubhouse, and more.

CRAFTY VISIONS HOLIDAY NEWSLETTER

http://www.wwvisions.com/newsletter/nov_dec97

Print directions to make the Mistletoe Doll, plastic canvas ornaments, gingerbread ornaments, and more.

"HOW TO MAKE A GINGERBREAD HOUSE" BY KAREN HAUGH

http://dinnercoop.cs.cmu.edu/dinnercoop/Recipes/karen/Gingerbrea dHouse.html

Read detailed directions on erecting a gingerbread mansion, which originally appeared in The Ottawa Citizen, *by Kathleen Walker.*

CLAY POT ANGELS

http://www.bfranklincrafts.com/angels.htp

Ben Franklin Crafts offers directions for making angels out of pots.

CHRISTMASTIME CELEBRATION HOMEPAGE
http://www.osmond.net/chill/christmas
This huge site from the Osmond Network contains 1,000 Christmas images, the words to more than 800 Christmas songs, plus stories, humor, and extensive links to other Christmas sites.

BEAD D'LIGHT PROJECTS FROM ENTERPRISE ART
http://www.enterpriseart.com/projects/beadlights/beadlight proj.html
You'll find directions for twelve bead projects designed to fit over regular Christmas lights. These projects are really cute and are a nifty way to decorate trees and wreaths.

HOMEPAGE FOR THE HOLIDAYS
http://www.merry-christmas.com
This site sponsored by 4CS is loaded with music, artwork, coloring books, games, and lots of activities for the entire family. You can e-mail Santa too.

CHRISTMAS COLORING PAGES
http://www.infocom.com/~hboyce/santa3.htm
Sandra Boyce and her family offer a holiday site with coloring pages and more.

Free Judaica Holiday Crafting Web Sites

TORAH TOTS: THE SITE FOR JEWISH CHILDREN
http://www.torahtots.com/holidays/rosh/roshstr.htm
http://www.torahtots.com/
Print coloring pages, and read stories at this lovely site from Reuven A. Stone.

HANUKKAH — NOT JUST FOR KIDS
http://www.night.net/kids/hanukkah.html-ssi

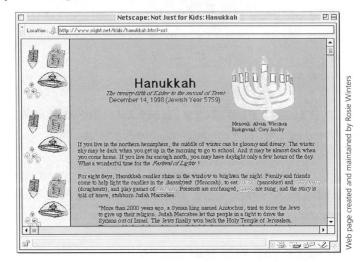

You'll find Hanukkah crafts, stories, games, and cards at this great site from Rosie Winters.

HAPPY HANUKKAH MENORAH
http://www.sewing.org/kidspage/menorah.html
Jo-Ann Fabrics & Crafts and the Home Sewing Association offer instructions for fashioning a colorful menorah.

Free Kwanzaa Crafting Web Sites

KWANZAA
http://www.afroam.org/children/fun/kwanzaa/kwanzaa.html
Learn about the history of Kwanzaa and the seven things most important at Kwanzaa.

KWANZAA WELCOME PAGE
http://www.globalindex.com/kwanzaa/welcome.htm
Learn how Kwanzaa began over forty years ago.

Free Valentine's Day Crafting Web Sites

BE MINE VALENTINE DAY CARD
http://www.fiskars.com/crafts/craft_projects/be_mine_card.html
Scissors-maker Fiskars offers directions for snipping a pretty card.

AMORE ON THE NET
http://www.holidays.net/amore/
Create and send a Valentine card, learn how Cupid became the Valentine symbol, and make a special Valentine.

VALENTINE'S DAY FROM THE TEEL FAMILY
http://www.teelfamily.com:80/activities/valentine

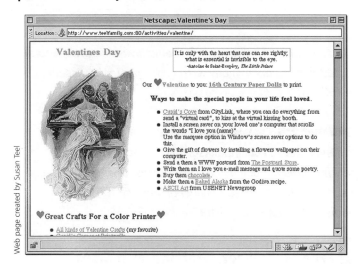

Lessons, trivia, and everything Valentine.

VALENTINE'S DAY FUN FROM THE KIDS EXCHANGE
http://www.netfix.com/poptart/valentin.htm
Find craft how-tos, recipes for finger-paint, modeling dough, and more.

Free Thanksgiving Crafting Web Sites

THANKSGIVING FOR THE KIDS
http://rats2u.com/thanksgiving/thanksgiving_kids.htm

You'll find a large selection of Thanksgiving-related web sites created for children, many with craft projects, assembled by the folks at St. Claire Associates.

A MUPPET'S THANKSGIVING
http://www.henson.com/thanksgiving
The Jim Henson Company offers games, crafts, and recipes. Be sure to check out the annual grudge match between Swedish Chef and Tom "The Turkey" Gobbler.

 Free Halloween Crafting Web Sites

HALLOWEEN CRAFTS
http://rats2u.com/halloween/halloween_crafts.htm
St. Claire Associates offers a huge collection of links to holiday projects including paper twist pumpkins, spooky fingers, and ghost wreaths.

HALLOWEEN TRICKS AND TREATS FROM NOT JUST FOR KIDS
http://www.night.net/halloween/

Web page created and maintained by Rosie Winters

Rosie Winters offers lots of Halloween goodies.

HALLOWEEN HOLLOW
http://www.bconnex.net/~mbuchana/realms/halloween/index.html
Marlene Buchanan of Canada offers ghostly fun and surprises, including directions for making bat puppets, spooky spiders, and owl invitations. You'll also find jokes, stories, Halloween party games, and decorations.

CARVING GREAT PUMPKINS FROM PACK-O-FUN
http://www.pack-o-fun.com/projects/pumpkin.htm
Here are illustrated directions on carving the Great Pumpkin. But get your parents to help!

HALLOWEEN MAGAZINE

http://www.halloweenmagazine.com

Here's a whole Web magazine devoted to Halloween! There are lots of craft projects, but also safety games and other activities.

MARY'S HAUNTED HALLOWEEN HOUSE FOR GHOSTS AND WITCHES

http://cgi.cadvision.com/~burke/halloween

"Abandon all hope ye who peruse these putrid pages," intones the "Old Witch Burke," also known as Mary. She offers creepy costumes, devilish decorations, and general foolishness.

 Free Easter Crafting Web Sites

UKRAINIAN EASTER EGGS

http://www3.ns.sympatico.ca/amorash/ukregg.html

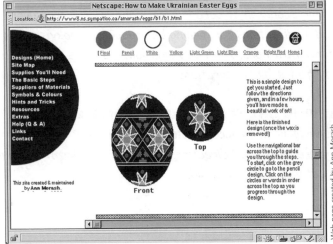

Ann Morash explains the basics of making pysanky, more commonly known as Ukrainian Easter Eggs.

THE HISTORY OF THE WHITE HOUSE EASTER EGG ROLL

http://www.whitehouse.gov/WH/glimpse/Easter/index.html

Read the history of the egg roll—how, when Congress forbade kids from rolling eggs on the Capitol lawn (they had made a mess in previous years), they were permitted to play on the White House lawn.

EASTER FUN AND GAMES

http://www.netfix.com/poptart/easter.htm

Wendy Hogan gives directions for woven baskets, bunny ears, and an Easter parade bonnet.

TWIN GROVES EASTER

http://www.twingroves.district96.k12.il.us:80/Easter/Easter.html

Learn how to decorate eggs, make Easter chicks, and more at this Twin Groves School District Web site.

Want to "Craft" with Mother Earth?

Visit these Web sites for inspiration for celebrating earth holidays—and planting trees.

EARTH DAY
http://falcon.jmu.edu/~ramseyil/holidays.htm

ENVIRONMENTAL LINKS—EARTH DAY
http://www.alexearthday.org/flink.htm

THE NATIONAL ARBOR DAY FOUNDATION
http://www.arborday.org

ARBOR DAY ONLINE
http://www.arborday.com

TIP

Send Free Greeting Cards to Your Friends

There are many Web sites where you can send free e-mail postcards to your friends. Tap into the site, select a card, add a message, and maybe select music too. The Web site will e-mail your recipient and tell them that a card is waiting for them. Here are some of our favorite card sites:

BLUE MOUNTAIN
http://www1.bluemountain.com

ELECTRONIC POSTCARDS
http://www.electronicpostcards.net/ecards.htm

DIGITAL POSTCARDS ON THE NET
http://www.advocacy-net.com/postcardmks.htm

free Stitching How-Tos for Kids

Kids love to sew. And they're never too young to learn. Five-year-olds can knit—maybe not correct, but they can have fun with the stitches. And who says a seven-year-old is too young to crochet? Or maybe you're an adult who just never learned to sew straight. Hey, these Web sites can help you, too. Pull out your safety-tipped knitting needles and crank up that toy sewing machine; you're about to learn to sew with the creative abandon of a kid.

SEWING FOR CHILDREN
http://www.ianr.unl.edu/PUBS/textiles/heg137.htm
Rose Marie Tondl of The Nebraska Cooperative Extension details what you need to know about fitting, measuring, and making children's clothing.

If You Need to the Learn the Basics of Sewing or Need a Refresher, visit the Mississippi State University Extension's 4H Clothing Project Reference Manual **(http://www.ext.msstate.edu:80/pubs/pub1302.htm).** This primer explains marking, measuring, sewing tools, hand sewing, clothing repair, the parts of a sewing machine, serging, pressing pointers,fabric, working with patterns, interfacings, seams, and caring for your clothes.

SEWING FOR LITTLE FINGERS
http://ctw.org/celebrate/athome/article/0,1439,7822,00.html
The Children's Television Workshop (masters of Sesame Street) show you how to make a lacing board using a paper plate and other household materials.

SUMMER SEWING WITH THE KIDS
http://sewing.about.com/library/blsumer.htm
Debbie Colgrove, the sewing guide at About.Com., offers links to projects for preschoolers, camp projects, and fundraisers.

HOME SEWING ASSOCIATION KIDS PAGE
http://www.sewing.org/kidspage/index.html
You'll find dozens of kid-friendly sewing projects at the cyber-home of the Home Sewing Association, including "bandanna pals," "bug jugglers," and "felted mug mats."

SEW YOUNG, SEW FUN: SEWING FOR TEENS BY HUSQVARNA VIKING

http://www.sewyoungsewfun.com

Wow! What a lot of cool sewing projects you'll find in the archives of this Web site! Stuff like free patterns for a "conversation heart swag" and "warm fleece mitts."

KIDS CAN STITCH PROGRAM

http://www.smocking.org

The Smocking Guild of America offers a program to help kids learn to sew.

KIDS CAN SEW

http://www.kidscansew.com/index.html

Learn how you can become a Kids Can Sew instructor.

YOUNG TEXTILE GROUP

http://www.hiraeth.com/ytg/welcome.htm

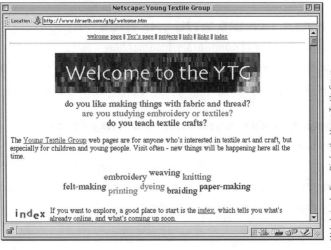

The Young Textile Group Web site is for anyone who's interested in textile arts and crafts, but especially children. Fiona Dix runs the site.

TEACHING KIDS HOW TO SEW
http://www.winonanet.com/mktplace/tvenette/teach.html
Theresa Venette explains how she teaches sewing skills to kids.

SEWING FOR CHILDREN
http://www.ianr.unl.edu/PUBS/textiles/heg137.htm
Rose Marie Tondl of The Nebraska Cooperative Extension details what you need to know about fitting, measuring, and making children's clothing.

QUILTING WITH CHILDREN
http://www.thecraftstudio.com/qwc/

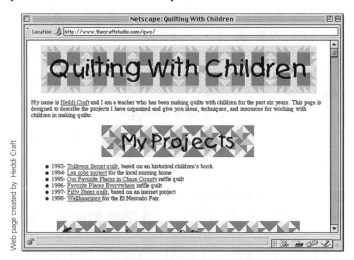

Heddi Craft, an elementary school teacher, describes quilting projects she organized for kids. Heddi offers techniques, ideas, and resources for making quilts with children.

THE WHO AM I QUILT PAGE
http://205.121.65.141/millville/teachers/carles/Carles94_95/Quilt/quilt.htm
This page describes the quilting curriculum Mr. Carles implemented in his fourth and fifth grade classroom in Millville, Utah.

QUILTING WITH CHILDREN, IDEAS AND INSPIRATION AT ABOUT.COM

http://quilting.about.com/library/weekly/aa072897.htm

Host Susan S. Druding offers a list of Web sites to help teachers and parents teach children to quilt.

YES, YOU CAN LEARN TO KNIT

http://www.skepsis.com/~tfarrell/textiles/knit/knitmain.html

Tom Farrell teaches the basics of knitting—good for all ages.

LEARN TO CROCHET

http://crafterscommunity.com/members/tutorials/crochet.html

You start by making a loop. There are complete instructions plus many illustrated projects for budding crocheters.

WONDERFUL STITCHING

http://www.needlework.com/

This is a Web site that stitchers of all ages can enjoy. You'll find all kinds of resources for cross-stitch, needlepoint, and other sorts of decorative stitching.

Visit These Web Sites for Free History Lessons on the Textiles of Our Ancestors

"MICHIGAN'S AFRICAN-AMERICAN QUILTERS" BY MARSHA MAC DOWELL AND LYNNE SWANSON

http://www.sos.state.mi.us/history/museum/techstuf/civilwar/quiltmag.html

"BLACK HERITAGE VIBRANTLY SHOWN IN QUILTS" BY JULIE STOEHR

http://www.dailyaztec.com/archive/1996/02/08/file005.html

NATIVETECH: NATIVE-AMERICAN ART AND TECHNOLOGY
http://www.nativeweb.org/NativeTech/

"THE HISTORY OF HMONG STORY CLOTHS" FROM THE MILWAUKEE JOURNAL-SENTINEL
http://www.hmongnet.org/culture/pandau.html

DAWN DUPERAULT'S TIMELINE OF QUILTING HISTORY IN AMERICA
http://www.redsword.com/dduperault/timeline.htm

Download Software for Kids Who Want to Sew Flash'N Fashion (**http://media-motion. com/flashn.htm**) offers a downloadable demo of their $19.95 software that helps youngsters learn to sew through sewing doll clothes. The software works on PCs.

Kidsew (**http://www.amouse.net/kidsew**) sells precut projects and kits for helping kids learn to sew.

Why Not Sew Up a Storm to Help Others? Click the "Stitches That Serve" icon on Viking's teen sewing Web site (**http://www.seyoungsewfun.com**) for information on teen sewing charity projects. Make "comfort caps" for childhood cancer patients or "cozy coats" for needy kids.

CHAPTER 17

Free
How-Tos for
Candlemaking,
Basket Weaving,
and Nature Crafts

The crafts of our forebearers satisfied desperate needs. They dipped candles because they needed light. They brewed soap because they needed to clean their skin after a hard day working in the fields. They wove baskets because they needed them to carry food. You'll find thousands of Web sites devoted to the crafts of our ancestors. The special supplies and the sometimes dangerous ingredients and tools needed (like lye for making soap) make it unwise for kids to try on their own the how-tos that are found on some of these sites. But these Web sites provide illuminating reading nonetheless. If you're interested in trying the crafts, print the Web page and give it to a parent or teacher.

Note! *Judy and Gloria would appreciate some "parental help" to make some of the things on these Web sites, like soap or candles. We don't want to set our kitchens on fire. Or our mother's kitchens either (sometimes they help us). If you want to volunteer, e-mail us. Kids, please, please don't try these things without a few helpful adults nearby! And a fire extinguisher.*

Free Nature Crafts How-Tos

NATIVETECH: NATIVE AMERICAN ART AND TECHNOLOGY

http://www.nativeweb.org/NativeTech/

© 1999 Tara Prindle

Tara Prindle runs this beautiful and informative site on the crafts and technology of Native Americans. You'll find tutorials on feather wrapping, porcupine quill decoration on birch bark, decorating pottery, finger weaving, and more.

NATURE CRAFTS FROM THE "GUIDEZONE" IN THE UNITED KINGDOM

http://www.guidezone.skl.com/nature.htm

You'll find directions for dozens of delightful projects including poinsettia napkin rings, leaf plates, and a kiwi fridge magnet.

KATHIE SCHMITT'S HERBAL CRAFTS PAGE

http://www.muscanet.com/~kschmitt/craft.html

Kathie offers directions for many projects that will sweeten the air of your pioneer's log cabin, including herbal wreaths, potpourri, and pressed herb candles.

"KINDER GARDENER" BY KAREN E. BLEDSOE

http://www.yard-garden.com

The Yard & Garden *magazine offers a regular feature on garden crafts for children, and you can read some installments at their Web site. Click "Kinder Gardener."*

THE GOURD ARTISTS GUILD

http://www.jkstacydesigns.com/GourdArtistsGuild.html

KID'Z GOURDZ

http://www.jkstacydesigns.com/kidzgourdz.html

If you've ever wanted to decorate a gourd, or create other art with squashes and such, this is the site for you. You'll find tutorials, links, a gallery of inspiration, and the history of gourd art in many different cultures.

 ## Free Basket Weaving How-Tos

BASKETRY AT ABOUT.COM

http://basketry.about.com/

Susi Nuss is your basketry guide at this wonderful site full of Web links, free articles, and links to how-tos and basketry directions around the Web.

BASKETS, ETC.

http://www.bright.net/~basketc/

Linda Braun offers lots of information about splint and reed basketmaking, gathered from basketmakers around the Web.

BASKET CLASS FREE PATTERNS

http://members.aol.com/basketclas/patterns.html

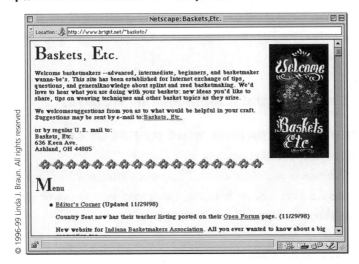

You'll find how-tos for a jelly caddy, cracker basket, and more. Click "Free Patterns 2" for more basket patterns.

NATIVE AMERICAN BASKETRY

http://indy4.fdl.cc.mn.us/~isk/art/basket/baskmenu.html

Paula Giese offers great articles on native basketry, plus links and photos.

WEAVER'S WORDS

http://www.iei.net/~davidc/

Join the Internet basket-making community. You'll find dyeing information, weaving tips, and more in its archives of past issues.

"BASKETWEAVING 101" BY ROBIN BONISCH

http://www.commnet.edu/QVCTC/student/BonischBasket/baskets. html

Robin offers an excellent introduction to basket weaving, plus history, references, and links to other basket-making sites on the Web.

 **BASKETRY!**

http://members.aol.com/basketry1/questions.html

*Linda Hebert of V.I. Reed & Cane answers questions about mak-
ing baskets from "What are baskets made out of" to "What are
'reed' and 'cane'?"*

 Free Soap and Candle-Making How-Tos

CANDLE AND SOAP-MAKING AT ABOUT.COM

http://candleandsoap.about.com/

*Bob Sherman is your host on this marvelous site, which offers
free projects each week, how-tos, chats, and links to candle and
soap-making sites around the Web.*

CANDLE MAKING

http://users.wantree.com.au/~campbell/candles.htm

*Sharon Campbell from Australia shares candle making instruc-
tions she's compiled in her twenty years as a candle maker. She
also offers free instructions for many projects.*

CANDLE MAKING AT THE CRAFTERS COMMUNITY
http://crafterscommunity.com/members/tutorials/candle.html
You'll find illustrated instructions, plus tips and project ideas.

🛒 HOW TO MAKE SOAP AND AROMATIC CANDLES
http://www.fast.net.au/wwalker/candles.html
Bill and Karen Walker from Amber Louise Essential explain how it's done.

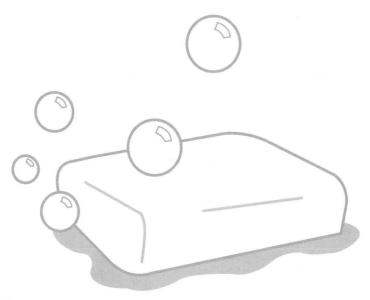

🛒 SOAP MAKING
http://www.soapcrafters.com
Learn how to make soap. Methods like "re-batch" and "melt and pour" are explained at this site by Soap Crafters.

WAXED OUT CANDLES AND CANDLE MAKING

http://www.vashti.net/WaxedOut/home.htm

You'll find some great candle-making how-tos and projects at the home of Waxed Out.

free Help for **Making** (and Repairing) Teddy Bears

W hen Margarete Steiff's nephew showed his famous German toymaker aunt the jointed bear he'd fashioned out of mohair, she pish-poshed it. She felt it was too expensive for children. But the nephew persevered and he sold a small order of bears to an American toy company. The bears, dressed as hunters and fishermen, soon found their way to the wedding table of Teddy Roosevelt's daughter as decorations, thanks to a clever caterer. When someone asked Roosevelt, who was famous for his hunting exploits, what species they were, he quipped "Teddy bears." (Since he was paying for the wedding, he was entitled.) And the Teddy bear legacy was born.

You'll find lots of kids and adults on the Web who make and love bears. You'll also find patterns and advice for assembling them, as well as repairing and caring for them.

Big Web Sites for Teddy Bear Makers and Lovers

Head to these Web sites to find inspiration, Teddy bear-making help, and fun.

TEDDY BEARS ON THE NET

http://www.tbonnet.com/second_index.html

Terry Bauman maintains this marvelous site full of book reviews, links to suppliers, Teddy magazines, museums, and discussion groups. You can buy Teddy bear-making kits, read Teddy design hints, and have a Teddy tell your fortune.

BEARWORLD!

http://www.bearworld.com

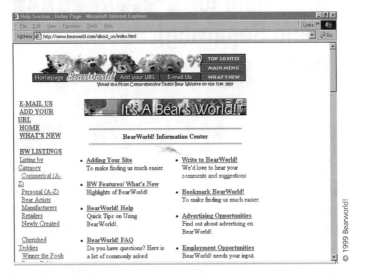

BearWorld! offers the biggest selection of Teddy bear links on the Net. You'll find advice on adding joints, selecting furs, and attaching eyes.

🛒 SPARE BEAR PARTS

http://www.SpareBear.com

This retailer of bear-making goodies offers a huge database of tips and how-tos on everything ranging from joint installation, furs, repairs, how to make a new bear look old and vice versa, needle sculpting, and installing music box keys. They also offer a free newsletter.

Free Teddy Bear Patterns

 THE TEDDY BEAR TIMES PATTERN ARCHIVE
http://www.teddybeartimes.com/patterns/listing.htm

This British magazine for lovers and makers of Teddy bears offers free downloadable patterns for bears, clothes, and accessories. They also offer information on suppliers and a Teddy bear chat.

 BEARLY HEAVEN
http://bluebonnetvillage.com/bheaven.htm

Cynthia Farrabee, a well-known bear maker, offers a gallery of her work. It will give you lots of ideas, and she includes a free pattern.

 BEAR MAKING TIPS FROM LABOURS OF LOVE
http://www.laboursoflove.com/p1293.htm

"When choosing your fur, remember shorter fur on smaller bears and longer fur on bigger bears." That's the sort of tip you'll find amid the compendium of bear crafting tips from Labours of Love.

BEARMAKING HINTS & TIPS FROM SHARINE DESIGNS
http://www.sharine.com/hints.htm

Bear pattern-maker ShaRine Designs of Alberta, Canada offers advice on Teddy bear fabrics, pressing, sewing, thread, and more.

Free Help for Bear Makers Who Give Bears to Those in Need

Maybe your local police or fire department already hands out Teddy bears to children facing trauma. If not, why not start a club to help them do it? Several organizations exist solely to dispense Teddy bears to children in need. Why not visit them to start your own Teddy "grassroots movement?"

GOOD BEARS OF THE WORLD

http://www.goodbearsoftheworld.org

This web page was created by Terri Effan

TEDDY CARE

http://www.teddycare.com

Doll artist Antonette Cely offers a free Bear Hugs Pattern (http://www.cely.com/bearhugs.html) for children in trauma. She has designed the bear to "hug" the child that holds him. The bear's arms wrap around the child's neck so that the bear's face presses against the child's cheek.

HOME SEWING ASSOCIATION "EMERGENCY BEAR" PATTERN

http://www.sewing.org/careshare/stuffdolls.html
http://www.sewing.org/careshare/teddybear.html

The HSA offers a simple stuffed bear pattern for a toy that emergency medical technicians can keep on hand in an ambulance.

free Help for Doll Makers and Lovers

N o one's ever too old to love a doll. Whether you need help fixing that Chatty Cathy that fell out of your bike basket one too many times, or you yearn to string red yarn hair on a Raggedy Ann, you'll find help and inspiration on the Web. You'll even meet artists who've made a name for themselves—and earn their living by creating beautiful dolls. You'll be amazed at the dollmaking—and fixing advice you'll find on the Web.

⭐ Big Web Sites for Dollmakers

If you're looking for help making—or you're just looking for other dollmakers to talk to, these are the places to go.

THE CLOTH DOLL CONNECTION

http://www.clothdollconnection.com
http://www.clothdollconnection.com/FreePatterns.html

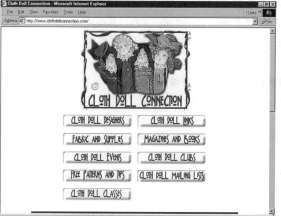

Karen Samuelson's Cloth Doll Connection is a fabulous site for dollmaking tips, links to free dollmaking patterns all over the Web.

This web page was created by Karen Samuelson

 DOLL NET
http://www.thedollnet.com

All dollmaking in cyberspace points toward Doll Net, where you'll find Web dollmaking supplies, shopping recommendations, free doll patterns, bulletin boards, chats, a mailing list, a gallery of dolls crafted by other cyber dollmakers, and much more.

CLOTHART
http://www.martydoll.com/index.html

Marty Donnellan's Web site offers tips and techniques, a mailing list for doll artists, a gallery of dolls, and some hard-to-find supplies for dollmakers.

DOLL STREET AT DOLLTROPOLIS
http://www.dolltropolis.com/dollstreet

Molly Finnegan's clever and witty site serves as cyber depot to dollmakers who just want to have fun making dolls. You'll find the Doll Street Dreams Doll Club, the Chatterer's Cafe & Carwash, the Doll Street Gazette, and much more.

MIMI'S DOLLMAKER'S PARADISE
http://www.mimidolls.com

Jim and Gloria J. "Mimi" Winer run this marvelous site which includes lots of doll photos, gossip on the professional world of dollmaking, and links to all the good doll crafting stuff on the Web. Plus you'll find Mimi's dollmaker's handbook, which is a treasure trove of good advice and direction.

DELPHI'S ARTIST DOLL FORUM
http://www0.delphi.com/artdolls

Web Sites of Dollmaking Magazines

THE CLOTH DOLL MAGAZINE
http://www.theclothdoll.com/index.html

You'll find some great how-tos—like one how to fashion life-like eyes—plus free patterns, and an archive of past features that appeared in this wonderful magazine.

Web site design: Internet Visions Company

DOLLMAKING & DOLL ARTISAN
http://www.DollmakingArtisan.com

Doll Artisan *is a magazine devoted to making porcelain dolls.* Dollmaking *is for makers of porcelain and sculpted dolls. You'll find a message board for dollmakers on this site—and sometimes you can snare a trial issue of one of the magazines.*

Travel the Doll Ring to Meet Other Doll Lovers. Like to surf the Web sites of other doll lovers? Head to the Doll Ring (**http://members. tripod.com/~hollie/dollring.html**). You don't need to "join" the ring to visit the Web sites linked by it. Just click on the logo to visit affiliated sites.

 **More Free Doll Patterns**

"MEGAN" DOLL PATTERN BY KAREN CUSICK

http://www.theclothdoll.com/megan.html

Karen offers illustrated instructions for sewing a 9" jointed doll with hair and a painted face. She also offers clothing patterns.

"COUSIN EZRA" FROM FAIRFIELD

http://www.poly-fil.com/crafts/CraftProject.html

Make a giant snail out of knits. This is a pattern the kids will enjoy, from poly-stuffing maker Fairfield.

CRAFTY VISIONS NEWSLETTER PATTERNS

http://wwvisions.com/newsletter

In its various issues, Crafty Visions offers occasional free doll patterns for things like a cupid doll and a fairy doll.

DOLL NET FREE PATTERNS

http://www.thedollnet.com

Doll Net offers a large directory of the Web sites of doll artists who offer free patterns on their sites.

DRACO THE DRAGON PIN FROM LEE MENCONI-STEIGER

http://members.tripod.com/~wingsnthings/draco.htm

Lee offers a pattern for a dragon you can pin on your blouse.

JOINTED BALLERINA BUNNY PATTERN FROM GAIL KELLISON

http://www.netins.net/showcase/dollpatterns/Freepattern2.htm

Everyone knows that bunnies were really intended to be ballerinas. Learn how to make reality confirm your imagination.

JUDI'S DOLLS

http://www.thedollnet.com/judi/index.html

Judi offers free patterns to sew a frog and an angel.

THE SWEATER GIRL FROM CASEY DOLLS

http://www.caseydolls.com/sweater.html

Dollmaker Jacqueline Casey offers directions for making an appealing doll out of an old sweater.

CHERUB PATTERN FROM GAIL'S STITCH N' SPLINTER PATTERNS

http://www.thedollnet.com/stitchnsplinter/index.html

Gail sells doll patterns but she also offers freebies.

ANGEL PATTERN FROM SISTERS & DAUGHTERS

http://www.sistersanddaughters.com/angel/index.html

Sisters & Daughters sells patterns and supplies but also offers freebies.

BUNNY PATTERN FROM THE PARCHMENT PRESS

http://hometown.aol.com/fabricdoll/frontpage.html

This publisher of doll and stitchery patterns offers a bunny pattern.

More Free Dollmaking How-Tos

MIMI'S HANDBOOK FOR DOLLMAKERS
http://www.mimidolls.com/handbook/handbook.htm
Gloria J. "Mimi" Winer offers advice on cleaning dolls; buying and caring for brushes; how to start a doll club; face painting; fabric; fashioning fingers, hair, and joints; needle sculpting, and more.

NOT JUST DOLLS GAZETTE
http://notjustdollmakers.com/gazette.html
This Web-zine from the Not Just Dolls mailing list includes regular features with tips and techniques on dollmaking.

CLOTHART TIPS AND TECHNIQUES
http://www.martydoll.com/Tips,Techniques.htm
Marty Donnellan offers some great techniques and advice—like how to harden a needle-sculpted nylon doll (so the nylon face doesn't run), and how to make wigs.

ANTONETTE CELY'S DOLL MAKING HELP

http://www.cely.com/doll.html

This world-renowned doll artist offers illustrated tips and tutorials on a variety of techniques, including how to properly fashion hands.

"HOW TO MAKE YOUR OWN DOLL BUTTONS" BY LEE MENCONI-STEIGER

http://members.tripod.com/~wingsnthings/button.htm

Lee offers directions for making your own attractive buttons from clay and other elements.

DOLLMAKING TECHNIQUES FROM CHIHARU KIKUCHI

http://www.asahi-net.or.jp/~eq5k-mgry/tech.htm

A Japanese artist offers illustrated techniques for sculpting doll faces.

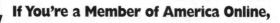

If You're a Member of America Online,

you can chat with other dollmakers in the Crafts & Needlework forum. Use the keyword SEWING. In the pop-up sewing menu scroll to the Sewing Board. (You'll need to scroll through the   message list to find the dollmaking discussions.) You'll find a small library of dollmaking patterns and pictures in the Crafts Community Library. Use the keyword SEWING and in the menu that pops up scroll down to and click on Crafts Community.

If you're a member of Compuserve, use the go

word SEWING to get to the Sewing & Quilting Forum. Scroll to the Dolls & Bears category. Click on Messages to chat with other doll and bear makers. Click Files to access a file library that includes a few free patterns, some bear-making tips, supplier lists and more.

Surf the Cloth-Doll Maker's Web Ring! Visit the

Web sites of other dollmakers by surfing this Web ring. Head to the links page at the Cloth Doll Connection (**http: //www.clothdollconnection.com/ClothDollLinks.html**). You don't need to join the ring in order to visit the sites.

Sew a "Dolly Hugs" for a Child in Need "Dolly

hugs" is a salutation used at the end of e-mail messages by many dollmakers, and it inspired doll artist Antonette Cely to design a special pattern for a doll to give children in crisis. Dolly Hugs' arms wrap around a child's neck and face, bestowing a little kiss. You can download the pattern for free from Antonette's Web site: The Dolly Hugs Pattern (**http://www.cely.com/dollyhugs.html**) to give to a child that needs a hug.

Join the Doll Collectors at the About.Com for Good Advice

You'll find great information on preserving dolls, caring for antique dolls, displaying dolls and more in About.Com's doll collector's forum (**http://collectdolls. about.com**).

Hunt for Dollmaking Notions, Patterns, and Clothes on eBay

You can find anything on the Web flea market site eBay (**http://www.ebay.com**). If you're a dollmaker you'll find patterns galore for dolls and doll clothes, especially vintage ones—everything from Barbie patterns to Holly Hobby patterns to clothing patterns for Betsy Wetsy. It's a motherlode of vintage doll patterns. We've seen patterns for clothes for French bed dolls from the '20s. You can find a lot of good things to embellish dolls with too—like vintage beads and plastic cameos (head to the "costume jewelry" category)—or old linens and lace. You can also find vintage children's clothing which can make ideal doll clothes, especially when embellished. To find all these we suggest using the Search feature on eBay's main page—the site is as large and jumbled as a giant fleamarket, with everything scattered everywhere. And check back every few days since items up for auction change so frequently.

ABOUT THE AUTHORS

Judy Heim

has been an avid needlecrafter for thirty years. She writes a regular column for *PC World* magazine, and she has written other articles for *Family Circle, C/Net, Newsweek, PC/Computing, Cosmopolitan,* and needlework magazines such as *Quilter's Newsletter Magazine* and *Sew News*. She is the author of four other books on needlecrafting and the Internet and co-author of the Free Stuff on the Internet Series. Judy lives in Madison, Wisconsin.

Gloria Hansen

has won significant awards for her quilts, most of which were designed using a Macintosh computer. She has written articles for computer magazines (including *Family Circle* and *PC World*) and for quilting magazines (including *Art/Quilt Magazine* and *McCall's Quilting*); she also writes the "High-Tech Quilting" column for *The Professional Quilter*. She has self-published patterns and her quilts have appeared in numerous magazines, books, and on television. With Judy, she is co-author of *The Quilter's Computer Companion* and co-author of the Free Stuff on the Internet Series. Gloria lives in central New Jersey.

BIBLIOGRAPHY

Heim, Judy and Gloria Hansen, *Free Stuff for Quilters*, C&T Publishing, Concord, CA,1998

_____. *Free Stuff for Quilters, 2nd Edition,* C&T Publishing, Concord, CA,1999

_____. *Free Stuff for Stitchers,* C&T Publishing, Concord, CA,1999

_____. *Free Stuff for Sewing Fanatics,* C&T Publishing, Concord, CA,1999

_____. *The Quilters Computer Companion,* No Starch Press, San Francisco, CA, 1998

Heim, Judy, *The Needlecrafter's Companion,* No Starch Press, San Francisco, CA, 1999

INDEX

adult craft projects 67

animation 22

antique macs 10

art, exploratorium 107

art, National Park Service
...........................103

art, Native American ..155

authors, web sites 64

balloon twisting 128

basket weaving ..154, 156

beading 120

bookmark, organize 17

bookmarks 16

bow making................135

browser 7, 9

browser, customize........16

browser, screening 35

browser, updating 10

bulletin boards 49

candlemaking..............154

Christmas crafting 136

clay, polymer 120

coloring pages 61

copyrighted pages 18

craft how-tos 43

craft stores 42

decoupage 114

dollmakers 165

dollmaking 165

Easter crafting 144

error messages 13

ftp 9

greeting cards 147

Halloween crafting 142

Hanukkah crafting 140

holiday craft 132

internet service provider ..7

ISP 7

jewelry making............120

Judaica crafting 19

juggling 129

kids care clubs 56

kids exchange................52

kite making 91

Kwanzaa crafting 140

lessons, art 104

lessons, drawing............99

lessons, painting............99

lessons, textile history..152

magazines, projects 40

magic 129

music 22

music, eyeneer archives
...........................107

nature crafts................154

navigating 15

network sites 65

origami.........................95

pages, saving to disk 19

paper airplanes.............88

paper dolls 84

paper dolls, printing 85

paper sculptures............77

paper, making 82

plug-in, downloading....28

plug-in, installing 28

plug-in, troubleshooting
...........................25

print pages 17

print, coloring pages 68

printer crafts.................83

puppet making............125

quilting........................151

rubber stamping..........108

safety 29-33

scrapbooking 111

searchers, safe 38

sewing basics 148

shortcuts, desktop 16

soap making 159

software, paper airplanes
...........................91

software, sewing 153

stains, removing 74

teddy bears 161

Thanksgiving crafting ..142

tole painting...............114

URL, definition 12

valentine crafting 141

virus 37

web page 11

For more information on other fine books from C&T Publishing, write for a free catalog:

C&T Publishing, Inc.,

P.O. Box 1456,

Lafayette, CA 94549

(800) 284-1114

http://www.ctpub.com

e-mail: ctinfo@ctpub.com

FREE STUFF ON THE INTERNET SERIES

Frustrated with spending hours of valuable time surfing your way around the Internet? C&T Publishing's Free Stuff on the Internet Series helps you quickly find information on your favorite craft or hobby. Our Free Stuff guides make it easy to stay organized as you visit hundreds of sites that offer all kinds of free patterns, articles, e-mail advice, galleries, and more. This series of handy guides lets you explore the Internet's infinite possibilities.

Free Stuff for Sewing Fanatics

Includes Web sites that offer free stuff for all kinds of sewing topics, including tailoring and fitting, sewing machine help, upholstery and draperies, home décor sewing, dollmaking, patterns and tutorials, heirloom vintage and bridal sewing, serging, fabric embellishment, and sewing for kids and pets.

Free Stuff for Quilters, 2nd Edition

The 2nd Edition of *Free Stuff for Quilters* includes over 150 updated new links on quilt patterns and tips, quilt discussion groups, guilds, and organizations, plus quilt shops to visit when you travel, how-tos for fabric dyeing, painting, stamping, photo transferring, and galleries of quilts, textiles, and fiber arts.

Free Stuff for Stitchers

Presenting an up-to-date list of sites that offer the best free stuff for stitchers! You'll find Web pages for knitters, machine knitters, cross-stitchers, plastic canvas stitchers, beaders, tatters and other lacemakers, spinners, weavers, braiders, knotters, tasselers, and bow-makers. More advice than you could read in a lifetime. This book is the stitcher's guide to the Internet's infinite possibilities.

www.ctpub.com